Universal Rights, Local Remedies

Implementing Human Rights in the Legal Systems of Africa

Papers and Proceedings of a Conference in Dakar, Senegal, 11-13 December 1997, on the Protection of Human Rights under the Constitutions of Africa, organised by INTERIGHTS, AFRONET and RADDHO.

Edited by Abdullahi Ahmed An-Na'im

INTERIGHTS
Afronet
GTZ

Co-Published by
INTERIGHTS
Lancaster House
33 Islington High Street
London N1 9LH
Tel: 0207 278 3230

Printed by
WCS Digital Print
Panther House
Mount Pleasant
London WC1X 0AN
Tel: 0207 278 0950

Design and Typesetting by
Jocelyn Lucas
Tel: 0207 284 3724

Illustration of African 16th Century Yoruba carved Ivory box
Courtesy of Rebecca Jewell

ISBN 1 869940 07 5
Price £18.00 / US $30.00

Contents

Acknowledgements

This book is a testament to unusual teamwork. The implementation of the project on which it is based has been made possible by the collaboration and enthusiasm of individuals, organisations and institutions from nearly fifty countries that inspired, supported and participated in the project. They are too numerous to mention individually here, but the contribution of each was essential for the success of this project.

One of the earliest supporters was Honourable Justice M. Ngulube, Chief Justice of Zambia, who addressed the planning meeting and facilitated its hosting in Lusaka, Zambia in July 1995. The success of the Dakar conference in December 1997 was due in large part to the hospitality and support of the hosts, Rencontre Africaine pour la Défense des Droits de l'Homme (RADDHO) of Senegal, and the able administration by Romana Cacchioli, Fauzia Shariff and Lisa Finch of INTERIGHTS and Dorah Chisambi of AFRONET. Lynn Muthoni Wanyeki not only contributed an essential media perspective to the project, but also undertook the difficult task of conference rapporteur, trying to convey the often technical legal discussions to non-lawyers.

The Board and Staff of AFRONET, and particularly its President, Olisa Agbakoba, provided invaluable support for the project through critical phases. From INTERIGHTS, Chidi Anselm Odinkalu has been the guiding spirit of the project throughout, and, together with Ibrahima Kane, has carried the burden of implementing the project. Emma Playfair and I have supervised and provided intellectual direction to all phases of the project.

The preparation and production of the publication has also been a collaborative effort among the staff of Interights and myself, ably coordinated by Romana Cacchioli. I am also particularly grateful to Sage Russell, of the Science and Human Rights Program of the American Association for the Advancement of Science, for her assistance with editing.

The project was generously supported by grants from the British Council, the Ford Foundation, GTZ (Germany), Norwegian Church Aid, NOVIB, and the Swedish NGO Foundation for Human Rights.

Abdullahi Ahmed An-Na'im
20 July 1999

In Memoriam

Hisham Mubarak

Hisham Mubarak, our colleague and companion in Dakar, died suddenly on 12 January 1998 at the tragically early age of 34. Although he died so young, Hisham had already made a notable contribution to the human rights movement in Egypt. As a young activist lawyer, who had himself been arrested and tortured, and in his work with the Egyptian Organisation for Human Rights, he brought immense dedication, courage, independence and professionalism to the defence of human rights. It was in recognition of these qualities that Hisham received the Reebok Human Rights Award, designed to recognise the contribution of young human rights activists, in 1993.

With the financial award he established a new organisation, the Center for Human Rights Legal Aid (CHRLA), which he directed until his death. Under Hisham's direction, CHRLA exemplified the approach that was under discussion in our meeting in Dakar, struggling to ensure that victims of human rights can look to the courts for protection of those rights under national constitutions and laws. CHRLA's network of lawyers developed a range of strategies to challenge violations of human rights before the Egyptian courts and to monitor the application of the law and constitution by those courts. CHRLA's strategies include advocacy before the courts, constitutional challenge of laws, critical analysis of proposed legislation, rigorous reporting of abuse of the law and critique of court decisions it believes open to criticism.

In Dakar, though inhibited by lack of confidence in his English from speaking in public, Hisham's comments in smaller groups were always notably thoughtful and insightful. He promised to expand on these in writing after his return to Egypt, and this report is undoubtedly the poorer for the fact that he was unable to do so.

Hisham's integrity, modesty, dedication and generosity in acknowledging the efforts of others touched all who knew him. He will be greatly missed not only in Egypt but by all his friends and colleagues elsewhere, including the many new friends he made in Dakar.

Emma Playfair
Executive Director
INTERIGHTS

MWANGI MBUTHIA

Mwangi Mbuthia, our colleague, friend and associate, was an early source of inspiration for the project on the legal protection of human rights under the constitutions of Africa. He was closely involved with the project from its conception in 1995 until his untimely death at the age of 34 years in December 1998.

To the friends of Mwangi Mbuthia - those that he grew up and schooled with as well as those he made over time - he was a truly exceptional person. Mwangi made friends easily and, above all, he was able to keep them. His friends transcended nationality, ethnic origin, class, sex and age. In Mwangi, we saw an unusual mixture of most of the qualities that we admire and aspire to be identified with.

He was firm in his convictions and opinions without being offensive or opinionated. He evenly blended humility with self confidence. He was humble and proud, without being a snob. He mixed seriousness and determination, with a great sense of humour that made that which was otherwise tedious and dull bearable. He was pleasantly eloquent and articulate as an advocate, activist, law teacher and stage actor.

As a practising advocate of the High Court of Kenya, we will always remember Mwangi for the public interest litigation that he handled free of charge for the Law Society of Kenya as well as the numerous briefs that he took up on behalf of indigent members of the public.

As the Secretary of the International Commission of Jurists (ICJ) Kenya Section, Mwangi ably and with commitment represented the organisation in many international functions and earned the respect and admiration of our Kenyan members as well as those of other national sections. From the time he joined the ICJ Kenya Section as a member soon after graduating from the University of Nairobi until his untimely death as the secretary, Mwangi was in the forefront in the activities, projects and programmes of the organisation, full of ideas and suggestions, and giving contributions in terms of his time and material support.

As friends and colleagues of Mwangi, we shall find eternal solace in the saying that 'no one is truly dead as long as he is remembered by someone'.

Katurima M'Inoti
Chair
ICJ, Kenya Section

Introduction

Abdullahi A. An-Na'im

This book contains four reports prepared under the auspices of a major multi-year project on the Legal Protection of Human Rights under the Constitutions of African Countries, co-organised by INTERIGHTS (The International Centre for the Legal Protection of Human Rights) and AFRONET (The Inter-African Network for Human Rights and Development). The project emerged in response to demands by African judges, human rights organisations, advocates and lawyers for greater awareness of existing mechanisms and institutions for the legal protection of human rights under African constitutions. However, as emphasised throughout this project, legal protections should neither be considered in isolation from the social, economic and political context of African societies in which they are supposed to apply, nor be assumed to be sufficient by themselves for the effective implementation of human rights standards. In other words, by focusing on legal protection, this project as a whole seeks to take a realistic yet visionary view of the practical possibilities and limitations of these mechanisms and institutions as part of a broad range of strategies for the implementation of human rights in African societies.

The activities undertaken under the auspices of this project, and reflected in the various chapters of this book, can be briefly described as follows. First, INTERIGHTS and AFRONET organised a planning meeting in July 1995, held in Lusaka, Zambia.[1] At that meeting, participants agreed on the need to commission studies of the norms, institutions, processes and general context of the legal protection of human rights in selected African countries for further discussion at an international conference to convene in an African country. That conference was held in Dakar, Senegal, in collaboration with Rencontre Africaine pour la Défense des Droits de l'Homme (RADDHO) on 11-13 December, 1997. To review and discuss follow-up activities after the Dakar conference, a small working group

---

1   An explanation of the background, organisation and various components of the project as a whole can be found in the report of that meeting: *The Legal Protection of Human Rights Under the Constitutions of Africa: Report of Planning Meeting, Lusaka, Zambia, 28 – 30 July 1995 ('The Lusaka Report')* prepared by Chidi Anselm Odinkalu. That report is on file at INTERIGHTS' offices in London.

convened on 15–17 May, 1998, at the offices of INTERIGHTS, London.

After clarification and further elaboration of the concept and rationale of the project as a whole, participants at the initial Lusaka meeting agreed on the criteria for the selection of countries to be studied.[2] They then developed a tentative list based on these criteria, pending further consultations about the selection and identification of authors of country studies. Briefly stated, the selection criteria sought to identify a representative sample of countries in terms of geopolitical factors, legal culture and system, regime of government, as well as the role of the state, and of customary/Islamic law. The countries selected for study at the Lusaka meeting and subsequently confirmed were Botswana, Egypt, Ethiopia, Guinea, Kenya, Morocco, Mozambique, Nigeria, Rwanda, Senegal, South Africa, Sudan, Uganda, Zaire (now Democratic Republic of Congo) and Zambia.

Authors were then identified and asked to organise their country studies under six headings: Introduction; Constitutional and Legal Framework for the Protection of Human Rights; the Judiciary and the Legal Profession; Political, Social and Economic Context; Status and Role of Non-Governmental Organisations; and Conclusions and Recommendations. As co-ordinator and editor of the forthcoming country studies, I sent detailed guidelines to each author indicating items to be included in each section, questions to be addressed and assessment of the role of each factor in the legal protection of human rights in the particular country. For example, I asked authors to begin with an overview of the historical background and demographic profile of the country, followed by the other sections in the above-mentioned sequence, and in as much conformity with the suggested content as possible. In their respective conclusions, authors were to provide an integrated and coherent evaluation of the current status and future prospects for the legal protection of human rights in the country studied. They were also requested to make practical and concrete policy recommendations, taking into account the realities described in the preceding sections. My primary concern in those guidelines was to ensure systematic and comprehensive coverage of similar subject-matter for comparative purposes, while allowing authors sufficient discretion regarding credibility of available information, manner and context of analysis, and evaluation of the content and role of each section in relation to the conditions and circumstances of the country in question.

Since it would have been costly and unwieldy to copy a complete set of country studies for each participant at the conference, and in view of the

---

2 The full statement of the selection criteria for the countries to be studied can be found in the *Lusaka Report*, p. 21.

fact that some studies were not received in good time for distribution, while some of those received were too tentative and incomplete, the organisers thought it better to try to inform and facilitate discussions at the conference through an introductory and synthesis paper. Accordingly, I prepared a paper in October 1997 for distribution prior to the Dakar conference, proposing a theoretical framework for discussions and incorporating a synthesis of the information obtained from those country studies received. That paper, as revised and updated after the Dakar conference, is now published as Chapters 1 and 3 of this book, Chapter 2 being the Keynote speech presented by Shirin Aumeeruddy-Cziffra. Unfortunately, I am obliged to say here, a few country studies did not sufficiently comply with the guidelines for providing useful contributions to the pre-conference synthesis. Moreover, some revised drafts were not subsequently received in good time for inclusion in Chapter 3 of this book. At the time of writing this Introduction, our effort is to ensure receipt of all revised and updated commissioned country studies for editing and publication in a major book.

Chapter 4 of this book is a report prepared by Chidi Anselm Odinkalu and Ibrahima Kane of INTERIGHTS on training and information resources for the legal protection of human rights in African countries, combining the work of two groups created by the Lusaka Planning Meeting. In order to avoid unnecessary duplication and build on existing resources and initiatives within and among various African countries, as well to explore ways of enhancing current collaborative efforts among African institutions, organisations and other actors in the field, the Lusaka meeting created two working groups.[3] One group was charged with assessing the nature and quality of existing information exchange among African NGOs, as well as formulating proposals for gathering, organising and disseminating legal developments about human rights in Africa on a sustainable basis. The second group was requested to assess and evaluate relevant training needs and facilities existing in Africa. The working groups subsequently merged into a single group.

In Chapter 5 of this book, L. Muthoni Wanyeki presents a thematic report of deliberations at the Dakar Conference of December 1997. Our purpose in including this conference report is to give readers a sense of the deliberations and conclusions of the conference. Because of the interactive nature of the programme of the conference, which deployed a mix of plenary sessions and discussion at small "break-away" groups, a formal

---

3   See Chapter 4, n.6 below, for the membership of the working groups.

presentation of proceedings in chronological sequence would have been artificial and misleading. Either means of presentation leaves something to be desired, but we hope that we have chosen the better way of sharing the insights and reflections of that highly successful conference.

Chapter 6 of this book presents a summary of the discussions and conclusions of the small working group convened on 15-17 May 1998 at the offices of INTERIGHTS to discuss possible follow-up activities to the Dakar Conference.[4] Although the meeting identified as concretely as possible follow-up activities to further the objectives and goals of the project as a whole, and assigned specific roles to the members of the working group, the purpose of that meeting was to set an agenda for action by whoever wishes to implement any aspect of those or other possible activities in furtherance of the legal protection of human rights in African countries.

In conclusion of this brief Introduction, I wish to gratefully acknowledge the editorial assistance of Sage Russell of Emory Law School, Class of 1997, currently Senior Program Associate at the Science and Human Rights Program of the American Association for the Advancement of Science. I am also most grateful for the useful comments and suggestions made throughout the preparation of this report by Chidi Anselm Odinkalu (Senior Legal Officer) and Emma Playfair (Executive Director) of INTERIGHTS.

---

4 The meeting began with a moment's silence observed in memory of Hisham Mubarak, Executive Director and founder of the Centre for Human Rights Legal Aid, Cairo, and a key contributor to the project, who died shortly after returning to Egypt from the Dakar Conference.

Chapter 1

Possibilities and Constraints of the Legal Protection of Human Rights under the Constitutions of African Countries

Abdullahi A. An-Na'im

This chapter was originally part of a report designed to present a synthesis of information obtained from all the country studies received by the organisers of this project prior to the Dakar conference of December 1997 in order to inform and facilitate discussions at that conference.[1] To introduce that thematic report, it was thought useful first to suggest a general theoretical framework for reflection and action under the mandate of this project. Although informed and influenced by the collective thinking of the Lusaka Planning Meeting of July 1995, and substantially based on the country studies received at the time of writing, this suggested framework is largely my own. But far from claiming to be definitive or exhaustive, these remarks are simply an attempt to place the analysis of the legal protection of human rights in various African countries in the broader context of struggles for human dignity and justice.

The proposed theoretical framework can perhaps serve as the basis for a common understanding and collaborative efforts in furtherance of the objectives of this project as a whole in the broader African context. Such a shared understanding is important if African human rights advocates are to pool their resources and draw on each other's strengths in effectively addressing common problems and concerns which may have the same or similar root causes despite the different manifestations in their respective societies. The challenge is to utilise the conceptual and practical commonalities of the struggles of African peoples in addressing specific country and regional situations through national as well as continental and global efforts.

It is true that the legal situation in each country should be studied on its own terms, and detailed strategies for the legal protection of human

---

1   The first draft of this report was written in October 1997 for the purpose of providing a synthesis of the country studies prepared prior to the conference which convened in Dakar, Senegal, 11-13 December of that year. That draft has since been revised in light of discussions at the conference, and updated to reflect some country studies not included in the first draft because they were not received by project co-organisers at that time.

rights should be developed and implemented in the context of the normative and institutional frameworks of the particular country. But the rationale of the present project is that such country-specific initiatives would benefit from insights gained from the experiences of other societies, as well as from an understanding of historical and current developments affecting all countries in Africa, as appropriate. Striving for the legal protection of human rights should be based on a clear understanding of the nature of the constitutional and legal orders under which such protection is supposed to materialise. This endeavour also calls for reflection on the relevance and efficacy of human rights in setting the normative standards of protection.

In my view, an appropriate theoretical framework for this continental initiative must mediate between two poles: the multi-faceted diversity of Africa on the one hand, and the similarity of the experiences of its peoples with colonialism and its aftermath, on the other. Due regard to the cultural, ethnic, religious, and other diversities of African societies counsels against generalisation. Yet the similarities of recent African experiences are too obvious and relevant to ignore in efforts to combine resources and develop responses to the far-reaching consequences of past colonialism and current globalisation.

In current usage, the term globalisation is used in several interconnected senses to refer to, *inter alia*, transformation of the relations between states, institutions, groups and individuals; the universalisation of certain practices, identities and structures; and the expression of the global restructuring that has occurred in recent decades in modern capitalist relations. Most recent definitions of this term emphasise global interdependence, flows and exchanges, the role of new technologies, the integration of markets, the shrinking of time and space, particularly the intensification of world-wide social relations. But as rightly observed by Tade Akin Aina, in such definitions 'there is a resounding silence with regard to the importance of notions such as coercion, conflict, polarisation, domination, inequality, exploitation and injustice.... [T]here is little or nothing about monopolies, disruptions and dislocations of the labour and other markets, the emergence of a global regulatory chaos and possible anomie and how these are being exploited for gains.'[2]

For the purposes of the legal protection of human rights in particular,

---

2   Tade Akin Aina, *Globalization and Social Policy in Africa: Issues and Research Directions* (Dakar, Senegal: CODESRIA Working Paper Series 6/96, 1997), 11.

such consequences include the establishment of European-model nation states premised on specific constitutional and legal assumptions, as well as the ways in which that model was misconceived or misapplied in African settings. They also encompass patterns of political development, educational systems and sociological trends, as well as economic, technological and other dependencies of African countries on the developed industrialised countries that have shaped the post-colonial experiences of African societies.

My proposal for mediating between the poles of African diversities and similarities in the present context is to focus on two unifying principles. First, as our subject is the legal protection of human rights, it is important to begin with an elaboration of the nature, rationale and utility of human rights as a normative basis for ensuring a humane and dignified life for all human beings. Second, since the legal protection of human rights is supposed to occur within national jurisdictions, as discussed below, one should consider the nature and limitations of current African states, which are charged with fulfilling this obligation. An analysis of these two unifying principles is necessary for identifying the basic issues and concerns with respect to the legal protection of human rights as defined in this project.

The Legal Protection of Human Rights in Africa

As a working definition at this stage of the analysis, I take human rights to be those claims which every human being is entitled to have and enjoy as of right by virtue of his or her humanity, without distinction on such grounds as sex, race, colour, religion, language, national origin or social group. The antecedents of these rights can be found in liberal notions of constitutional civil liberties as protection against abuse of power by the state, hence the notion of a *negative* obligation on the state to refrain from action that violates these rights. But the modern concept of human rights should include an affirmative *positive* obligation for the state to act in the implementation of these rights as well as the negative sense of refraining from action that violates them. This generally accepted definition does not provide an authoritative list of what these rights are, nor specify the precise content of any right in particular. It does not even address the issue of criteria and methodology by which specific human rights can be identified and recognised. For example, it does not settle the controversy about the standing and efficacy of economic, social and cultural rights, or whether there are collective human rights other than the right to self-determination. I will return to the issue of definition and content later on, after addressing the questions of how and by whom human rights are to be respected and protected, whatever they may be. To propose a theoretical definition and enumerate a list of human rights in the abstract, without first clarifying the process by which these rights are supposed to be implemented, might be seen as an exercise in wishful thinking.

The basic concept of human rights as claims to which all people are entitled as of right by virtue of their humanity firmly locates these rights and their implementation in the social and political realm of human affairs. Whatever these rights are, their implementation will necessarily require collective and sustained efforts that require the allocation of resources over extended periods of time. The realisation of human rights also presupposes the existence of an authority that can mediate among rights in case of conflict and adjudicate the competing demands of claimants of rights. Therefore, the basic concept of human rights can only be realised through some form of wide-scale political organisation that is capable and willing to undertake these functions. The state is the form of political organisation that is universally established today, indeed assumed by the present system of international human rights. This reality not only involves the apparent paradox of expecting the state to vindicate human rights against its own organs and officials, but also to be able to act affirmatively in the implementation of these rights. What is the nature of the state in Africa, and how is it likely to fulfill these multiple roles of promoting and protecting human rights?

Whatever its failings and problems may be, as discussed in the next section, it should be noted that the post-colonial state in Africa is not only likely to remain the most viable regime of political organisation for the foreseeable future, but it can also be transformed to better serve certain functions. Though traditionally contested by a variety of cultural (customary) institutions and networks, and increasingly undermined by globalising forces, the state remains a fundamental framework for political interaction, social relations, economic development, administration of justice, and provision of essential services at the national level. It is also the entity recognised and dealt with by all other states and external actors on such matters as international trade and economic activities, and foreign relations. By virtue of its juridical sovereignty under international law, the nation state is the universally acknowledged medium of policy formulation, decision-making and action. In short, it is the embodiment of national sovereignty as the supreme political organ of society.

For the purposes of this project in particular, it should be emphasised that the very concept of legal protection of human rights assumes and presupposes the existence of the state as the source of authority for the normative framework as well as of the institutional capacity needed for such protection. That is clear enough with respect to national constitutional and legal systems, as well as human rights norms and implementation mechanisms based on international treaties between states. Even principles of customary international law, to the minimal extent that they establish human rights norms,[3] are premised on state practice out of a sense of legal obligation. It is true that formal legal obligations and implementation mechanisms are supported by such informal methods as pressure by non-governmental organisations and the media or by diplomatic exchanges. However, these international efforts seek implementation of human rights obligations through legislation and enforcement by national jurisdictions, and not by direct action independent of the will of the state in question.

Therefore, whether at the national or international level, the state is the legal entity that determines the standards and implements them. To the extent that human rights are provided for at the national or domestic level in a country's constitution or legal system, or as a result of international legal obligations, the juridical sovereignty of the state presupposes that its appropriate organs and institutions have exclusive jurisdiction (at least nominally) over the interpretation and implementation of those rights. From this perspective, the central role of the state is obvious, and the issue of how

---

3   Human rights principles presently established as a matter of customary international law include the prohibitions on slavery, genocide and torture. In addition to the difficulty of proving the existence of principles of customary international law in general, the nature and dynamic of this source of international law are not conducive to precise specification of legal norms nor to their effective implementation. But see 12 *INTERIGHTS' Bulletin,* 5-7 for a discussion on determining the extent to which elements of the Universal Declaration of Human Rights may be now considered to constitute customary law.

to ensure state compliance with its own constitutional and legal norms is discussed below. But since most African national systems do not normally provide for a wide range of human rights, and as the term is much more closely associated with internationally recognised rights, regardless of their presence or absence in national domestic systems, further elaboration on what happens at the international level is necessary.

From that external or universal point of view, the present international standards of human rights were negotiated and adopted by delegates of state governments, and became binding as treaties between states. Under international law, treaties create international obligations, but each state has the ultimate power to interpret and implement them within its own exclusive national jurisdiction, although other actors may try to influence state action in this regard. Inter-governmental organisations like the United Nations and its organs, non-governmental organisations, the media and public opinion, and other actors seek to influence the human rights performance of various states. These activities are most welcome, and indeed essential for the respect and protection of human rights. But the point to emphasise here is that such efforts can only work through the agency of the state, and not by means of independent action within the territory of the state without its cooperation or at least consent.

Because the present international human rights standards derive their validity and binding nature from treaties, it is important to note the implications of that fact for the implementation of these rights. As a matter of international law, a state owes its legal obligations to other states parties to the treaty, and those obligations are normally vindicated through interactions among states (and often with intergovernmental organisations like the United Nations as well, which may be parties to such treaties). If other states parties deem a state to be in breach of its obligations, it is up to those states to take the necessary action under international law to ensure compliance or otherwise retaliate against the offending state. As a general rule, the whole system does not conceive of any legal role for non-state actors, although they may well be able to exercise strong political or other influence on state actors.

However, this system and its assumptions do not work well for human rights treaties because their beneficiaries are individual persons and groups making claims against the state, the entity that is supposed to represent them in the international arena. Other states who are party to a human rights treaty are unlikely to seek legal enforcement of these treaties against an offending state which is a party to the same treaty because the protection of human rights is not normally accepted as a sufficiently compelling interest for them to risk their relations with the offending state. In other words, a state may have a sufficient sense of self-interest to pursue a breach of international obligations by another state in, for example, trade and economic relations, defence and national security matters, or fisheries and other natural resources. States may also deem protecting their nationals from the actions of other states to be part of their self-interest, although they may not be able to provide that protection effectively in some situations. No state, however, is likely to risk its own self-interest to challenge another state's failure to honour its international human rights obligations to its own nationals. It is not surprising, therefore, that the state complaint procedures are rarely if ever used, even against states that are universally condemned for their flagrant and massive violations of human rights standards.

It is true that there have been some recent attempts by a few states to include human rights concerns in their foreign policies and international relations through political conditionality of aid, diplomatic pressure, or even as part of the rhetoric of justifying so-called humanitarian intervention. But the motives of those states are so mixed and suspect, and their foreign policy interests are so complex and varied, that this can hardly be taken as a reliable device for the protection of human rights in other countries. In any case, responses by other states are too slow, inconsistent and generalised to assist specific individual or group victims of human rights violations.

In this light, it is clear that it is the individuals and groups who are the beneficiaries of human rights standards themselves who have to act to protect their own rights, whether against their own state, or by inducing it to support them against external actors or conditions causing the human rights violation.[4] This is necessary whether the source of these rights is a national constitution and legal system, or international treaties that are ratified and incorporated into the domestic legal system. It may sound odd

---

4   It should be noted that all persons and groups are 'beneficiaries' of human rights standards, not only the immediate victims of violations. Indeed, violators too can become victims when they fall out of favour with an oppressive government they have served in the past, or when there is a revolutionary change of regime.

to speak of the victim as protecting his or her rights, but that is in fact true in all cases, whether on the international plane where other states are motivated to act out of self-interest, or at the national level where individuals and groups are also normally motivated by self-interest. The initial question in each case concerns the relative power relations between the violator and victim: what relative advantage or leverage point does the victim have to oblige the violator to comply? Part of the answer to this initial question can be found in the availability of effective means of recourse for the victim, which the violator will find difficult to resist. But the main issue is how to shift the balance of power in favour of the victim to enable him or her to change the behaviour of officials of the state, or cause the state to respond to some other source of human rights violation.

Focusing on the legal protection of human rights in national settings in particular, the first point to make is that being a victim does not necessarily mean that one is standing in an objectively and permanently weaker position in relation to the violator. In fact, the violator's power is usually dependent on the actual or potential victim, and derives from the victim's perception of the situation. Whenever the actual or potential victim refuses to submit to the apparent power of the violator, and considers the situation in terms of what he or she might be able to do in resistance, the terms of the relationship between victim and violator have already begun to shift. Part of that transformation lies in an understanding of the balance of power relations between the victim and the violator, and how that balance might shift sufficiently in favour of the victim to prevent the violation in the first place, as well as in knowledge of effective forms of redress for the harm done to the victim.

The psychological dimension of this relationship is closely linked to its political dynamics, because neither violators nor victims exist in a political vacuum or are likely to act without evaluating the consequences of their actions, especially in terms of the reactions of actual or potential victims. This is as true for the state as it is for any private actor or other entity. Despite all its material manifestations and the coercive resources available to it, the power of the state is first and foremost political, and resides in the willingness of its population to accept or at least acquiesce to its actions. In fact, the state itself is a political creature because it does not have an existence independent of the people who control its apparatus and accept its commands. Because those in control of the state are a small fraction of those who accept its power, the small minority must have a way of persuading or inducing the vast majority that it is in their best interest to accept the commands of those in control of the state. In fact, not a single government in the world today would claim that it is entitled to rule without regard to its ability and willingness to serve the best interests of its population. In my view, that makes the best interest of the totality of the population the *raison d'être* of the state as a political institution.

At first glance, there may appear to be several possibilities for sustaining the political authority of the state, including the force of tradition or the moral or religious standing of those in control of its apparatus. Political authority may even appear to be founded on the reality of effective control over the population through sheer force of intimidation. But in fact, all these possibilities are simply manifestations of the same phenomenon: that is, that the population at large is accepting (or acquiescing to) the authority of those in control of the state. Since human beings are always motivated by their interest in basic survival as well as by their material and moral well-being, the decision to accept or submit is usually based on people's belief that the choice they make is in their best interest. Whatever may be the apparent bases of its authority, people will not submit to policies and actions that threaten their fundamental self-interest in human existence. The phrase 'human existence' indicates that more is at stake than purely physical survival, and it incorporates a sense of social justice and human dignity. Resistance may be delayed in proportion to the psychological force of the bases of authority, as when people are culturally conditioned to accept the command of traditional or religious leaders. But resistance will also mount in response to increasing threats to people's self-interest, ultimately undermining the credibility of such leaders. Even when people submit out of fear for their personal safety, I believe that there will come a point when the drive for human existence, as defined above, will overcome the force of intimidation by those in control of the state.

In this light, I would conclude that the strength of a people's political will to insist on respect and protection of their human rights is correlated to their belief that those rights are essential for their human existence. In other words, I suggest that weakness in a people's determination to resist violations of a certain set of human rights indicates a lack of conviction that those rights are essential to their human existence. Conversely, the stronger this conviction, the more likely it is that people will insist that the state respect and protect those rights against anyone who violates them. The question that emerges from this analysis is whether any particular set of human rights has attained, or is likely to attain, this degree of adherence among the purported beneficiaries.

It should be noted here that this question is relative in the sense that the strength of a people's willingness to accept the consequences of resistance is proportional to their beliefs about the relationship between a given right and human existence. For example, people will more readily resist a threat to their physical survival than denial of their right to participate in their own government or violation of their freedoms of expression or association, which appear abstract and far removed from their daily concerns. These two different reactions to perceived threats in terms of the relationship between such freedoms and physical survival are also relative. Denial of the right to participate in government is likely to be resisted to the extent that it is believed to be related to physical survival, as when bad economic planning or inadequate response to natural disasters causes threats to human life or essential health. The matter is relative in that it does not necessarily follow that people will only resist life-threatening violations, even though they are unlikely to risk their lives if they believe that relatively little is at stake. The question in the present context is therefore: how do African peoples understand human rights and perceive the relationship between those rights and their own human existence?

The norms that have come to be known since the middle of this century as 'human rights' certainly had philosophical, religious and intellectual antecedents in the history of many societies. Furthermore, the values and institutions which underlie these norms have also been accepted by many societies in a variety of ways. In that sense, one can speak of the universality of human rights as a product of commonalities in the human experience of civilisation and widely accepted moral insights. But the idea of legal enactment of these norms as overriding constitutional rights clearly emerged from Western political and intellectual experiences. During the last two centuries, and especially since the beginning of the twentieth century, these rights have come to be written routinely into constitutional bills of rights in many parts of the world, including those of most African countries upon independence. While the constitutional origin of human rights should be noted, the term 'human rights' is more appropriately applied to the international norms that became the model - in scope and formulation - for most African and other constitutions. Since the adoption of the Universal Declaration of Human Rights in 1948 and the various specialised covenants and conventions that followed, the most important developments in the international human rights system have occurred under the auspices of the United Nations.[5]

The apparent problem with the constitutional origins and the international development of human rights from the point of view of African societies is that they were not an integral part of either process. At the time that written constitutions with bills of rights originated, African societies were not organised as nation states and therefore did not have their own constitutions. When the international human rights system originated, with the adoption of the Universal Declaration, drafted under the auspices of the UN, only four African countries were members of the United Nations (Egypt, Ethiopia, Liberia and apartheid South Africa). These origins and early developments came to influence post-independence constitutional enactments and practice, as well as the conception and drafting of the African Charter on Human and Peoples' Rights. Moreover, the concept of the nation state, with its constitutional order and bill of rights that African societies were supposed to adopt after independence, was a colonial imposition and not the product of internal political, social and economic developments. This is one reason for the perception in African societies that human rights lack legitimacy.

A second dimension of the legitimacy issue is the apparent tension between some African cultural and religious traditions and certain human rights norms, especially with respect to the human rights of women,

---

5   The adoption of the African Charter on Human and Peoples' Rights in 1981, and its coming into force in 1987, provides a regional focus for activities under the auspices of the Organisation of African Unity. But the interpretation and application of the African Charter should draw upon the international and other regional (European and Inter-American) systems, rather than an isolated, purportedly exclusively 'African', effort, and vice versa.

children and minority groups. Similar tensions exist within all societies, including Western societies, with respect to these or other human rights. The United States, for example, has had great difficulty accepting social, economic and cultural human rights as such. However, these tensions seem to be more pronounced in African societies, not only because of the legitimacy issue with respect to the origins of the international human rights system, but also because at the time these societies lacked sufficient political stability and economic development to resolve such issues for themselves. Moreover, both legitimacy issues have been exaggerated in the African context through deliberate manipulation by those who wish to discredit and marginalise the human rights paradigm altogether for their own political or ideological reasons. Opponents of human rights in Africa include ruling elites seeking to legitimise their authoritarian regimes and oppressive practices, as well as religious fundamentalists and other cultural relativists, who perceive the human rights ethos as antithetical to their world view and vision of the good society.

Proponents of human rights in Africa should take seriously these challenges to the legitimacy of human rights in African societies. Human rights advocates should not assume that the majorities in their respective societies already understand and accept these norms, but do not uphold them in practice solely because of oppressive regimes or authoritarian social structures and institutions. Instead, Africans may be failing to stand up for their human rights because they do not view them as essential to their human existence, rather than because they are unwilling to suffer the consequences of insisting on the protection of these rights. While emphasising the seriousness and difficulty inherent in resolving these legitimacy issues, I strongly believe that it can be done if human rights advocates in Africa make it a high enough priority.[6]

In considering why to pursue a strategy of legal protection of human rights in particular, it is important to emphasise that the very concept of human rights in the modern sense of the term is that these are entitlements *as of right,* and not simply because of charity, social solidarity or other moral considerations, although those purposes may also be served in the process. In the present context of state societies in Africa, in contrast to what they

---

6 On these issues, see generally, Abdullahi Ahmed An-Na'im & Francis M. Deng, eds., *Human Rights in Africa: Cross-Cultural Perspectives* (Washington DC: Brookings Institution, 1990); and Abdullahi Ahmed An-Na'im, ed., *Human Rights in Cross-Cultural Perspectives: Quest for Consensus* (Philadelphia, PA: University of Pennsylvania Press, 1992).

may have been in pre-colonial times, for a human right to be a matter of entitlement, there has to be a legal mechanism to implement or enforce it, when necessary or appropriate. Whatever other strategies may exist for the promotion and protection of human rights, there must be ways and means to protect them legally if human rights are to be rights at all.

The legal protection of human rights serves two valuable functions. First, if effective forms of legal protection are available, people have the means to resist violations of their rights peacefully and in an orderly fashion, without having to risk their personal safety or suffer other serious consequences. The availability of this option helps shift the balance of power in favour of victims – actual or potential – and against the violator. The victim's apprehension that the cost of resistance might be too high is part of the violator's psychological advantage. Reducing and quantifying the consequences of resistance by utilising legal process reduces this psychological advantage of the violator over the victim. In addition, the legal processes are themselves a form of practical support to the process of resistance.

The second useful function of the legal protection of human rights is that it provides society with opportunities to resolve conflicts within particular rights or between competing claims of rights. The deliberate nature and slow pace of the legal process are highly conducive to the sort of philosophical and sociological reflection needed to resolve difficult issues, such as where and how to strike a balance between freedom of speech and the protection of one's privacy and reputation. For example, should the incitement of racial or religious hatred, commonly known as 'hate speech', be allowed, out of respect for freedom of opinion and expression, or prohibited because of its negative social and political consequences?

An appreciation of the legal system's valuable functions in protecting human rights will help to build political support for this avenue of redress. Other sources of political support are needed as well because of the variety of preconditions to be met in order for legal protection methods to succeed. Strong political support is needed to ensure that the legal protection approach receives sufficient human and material resources for its effective implementation. An understaffed and overcrowded legal process is hardly conducive to social and moral deliberation over difficult issues of policy.

Even stronger political support is needed to demonstrate to those in control of the apparatus of the state that there is no way of escaping legal accountability for failure to comply with human rights norms.

The first precondition for building political support for legal protection of human rights is the recognition that it cannot be taken for granted or assumed to exist. Strategies for generating this political support include conducting public awareness-raising campaigns on the importance and benefits of legal protection, and stimulating the favourable public opinion and momentum needed to increase the chances of success for the legal protection of human rights when invoked by actual victims seeking legal redress.

As I suggested at the outset, examining the nature and function of the African state is useful in developing a theoretical framework for this project on the legal protection of human rights. The concept of the state is one of the unifying themes of the project, serving as an effective means of bridging the gap between the similarity in the overall patterns and the diversity in the individual details of the African experience. I will now turn to a brief discussion of the nature and operation of the state in Africa, particularly in relation to the underlying issues in the legal protection of human rights.

The Post-Colonial State in Africa

Despite the wide diversity of earlier African systems of social and political organisation, and notwithstanding significant differences in their colonial experiences, all African societies today live under the European-model nation state. Even countries like Egypt and Ethiopia, which were not colonised in the formal sense of the term,[7] have come to adopt the same European model in order to gain national sovereignty and international recognition. Paradoxically, even though a poor copy of an alien model imposed by European colonialism, and incapable for a variety of reasons of discharging its responsibilities at home and abroad, the post-colonial state in Africa is supposed to enjoy all the prerogatives and privileges of equal sovereignty. African states are expected to protect their citizens and territories, and to that end are considered to be entitled to exclusive national jurisdiction over them.

---

7 Egypt was greatly influenced by France following an invasion by Napoleon around 1802, and was subsequently occupied by Britain in 1882 as a 'protectorate'. Ethiopia was briefly occupied by Italy during the 1930s, and had to cope with considerable European interference in its internal affairs. However, both countries retained their own native monarchies until they were overthrown by national revolutions in 1952 in Egypt and 1974 in Ethiopia, and were never colonised in the same way suffered by other African societies.

As explained by Jackson and Rosberg, although many African states are internally deficient and externally weak, their sovereignty is guaranteed by the world community of states in ways that stand in sharp contrast to the 'classical historical pattern [of Europe] in which external recognition is based on empirical statehood, usually achieved in alliance with other states under strenuous conditions of international rivalry.'[8] As a product of European experiences in state formation and nation-building, modern international law came to embody Eurocentric concepts of sovereignty and standards of civility as conditions for the recognition of states. Other parts of the world which failed to qualify for full membership at the time, including virtually all of Africa, became vulnerable to European colonisation and its consequences, which meant accepting the imposition and functioning of the post-colonial state. Jackson and Rosberg explain the situation clearly and succinctly as follows:

> African states are direct successors of the European colonies that were alien entities to most of Africa. Their legitimacy derived not from internal African consent, but from international agreements - primarily among European states - beginning with the Berlin Conference of 1884-85. Their borders were usually defined not by African political facts or geography, but rather by international rules of continental partition and occupation established for that purpose. Their governments were organised according to European colonial theory and practice (tempered by expediency), and were staffed almost entirely by Europeans at decision-making levels. Their economies were managed with imperial and/or local colonial considerations primarily in mind. Their laws and policies reflected the interests and values of European imperial power, and these usually included strategic military uses, economic advantage, Christianisation, European settlement, and so forth. Although the populations of the colonies were overwhelmingly African, the vast majority of the inhabitants had little or no constitutional standing in them.[9]

---

8   Robert H. Jackson & Carl G. Rosberg, 'Sovereignty and Underdevelopment: Juridical Statehood in the African Crisis', 24 *Journal of Modern African Studies*, vol. 24, (1986), 2.

9   Op. cit., 5-6.

Ironically, the same African entities that were deemed unqualified for sovereignty until the eve of their independence, were suddenly propelled into full sovereignty through the process of decolonisation. Yet, African societies had little control even over the timing and dynamics of the process of decolonisation that was supposed to 'restore' their sovereignty. Independence eventually came about as a result of shifts in the dynamics of European domestic politics and international relations after the Second World War. The timing of independence was largely decided by the colonial power based on its own considerations, rather than by internal developments within African societies. In order to end immediately the colonial oppression and exploitation of African societies, the 1960 United Nations Declaration on the Granting of Independence to Colonial Countries and Peoples stipulated that 'inadequacy of political, economic, social or educational preparation should never serve as a pretext for delaying independence.' However, the practical consequence was that, 'by the late 1950s, under increasing international moral and political pressures, the juridical right of self-determination has been separated from the empirical capacity for self-government in decolonisation.'[10] This blanket and unconditional preservation of juridical statehood and territorial integrity, regardless of a state's ability and willingness to live up to the national and international obligations that follow from it, has been the primary concern of the Organisation of African Unity since it was established in 1963.

This preoccupation with the preservation of juridical statehood does not mean that African countries are free from serious political conflict. The sovereignty and stability of African states are constantly contested in regional conflicts and internal civil wars,[11] as well as by diminishing control over vital national economic and social policy under current structural adjustment programs and unfavourable global trade relations. Such serious threats have led African states to be more concerned with their juridical sovereignty and political stability at almost any cost than with their ability to perform the essential functions of protecting and serving their citizens.

Another significant factor worth noting here is the nature of colonial administration and the political culture it cultivated in African societies. For decades, colonial powers exercised exclusive control over local populations

---

10 Op. cit., 9.

11 Regional conflicts have ranged from Tanzania's invasion of Uganda to overthrow Idi Amin in 1978-79, Morocco's forcible occupation of large areas of the Western Sahara since 1976, the Ethiopian/Somali wars of the 1970s and 1980s, and invasions and destabilisation tactics by apartheid South Africa against neighboring countries until the early 1990s, to the current conflicts in the Great Lakes region of Central

by ruling through a few educated local elites and traditional rulers and by the extensive use of divide and rule tactics. All that independence signified in most African states was the transfer of control over authoritarian power structures and processes of government from colonial masters to local elites. Notions of popular participation in governance and the diffusion of authority and power at the national level were never known to African societies during colonial rule or after independence. The political parties established during the struggle for independence often remained auxiliary institutions of personal power, and were rarely transformed into authentic organisations of public opinion or expressions of popular sovereignty.

Moreover, with external defence secured by agreements among colonial powers, beginning with the Conference of Berlin and largely preserved by the OAU since 1963, state security came to mean directing military forces inward at African populations as protection against rebellion or riot. National security came to signify the security of the regime in power, with no possibility whatsoever of transparency, or political or legal accountability in the operation of the security forces. Unable to govern effectively and humanely, post-colonial governments tended to compensate by using oppressive and authoritarian methods, usually employing the same colonial legal and institutional mechanisms maintained by several cycles of 'native' governments since independence.

Finally, since the state usually lacked an effective presence in most of its territorial jurisdiction, ruling elites tended to focus on controlling the government apparatus and patronage system, striving to retain the support of key ethnic leaders, instead of seeking genuine legitimacy and accountability among the population at large. Ironically, those shortsighted political strategies in fact contributed to the loss of power by most of the first generation of civilian African leaders to military usurpers who succeeded in controlling the government and the country as a whole, simply by physically seizing a few officials and key government installations in the capital. Within hours of a successful coup, military usurpers would be considered to be in 'effective control of the government', and would therefore be granted automatic recognition by 'the international community' in almost every instance. In this way, both the domestic and

Africa. Many African countries have also suffered devastating civil wars, some continuing for many decades, as in Sudan, or in several cycles, as in Chad.

international sources of recognition of independent statehood in post-colonial Africa have tended to be exclusively concerned with the sovereignty of the government, and not of the people.

Of particular significance to the legal protection of human rights is the general weakness of the principle of constitutionalism itself in most African states,[12] and the failure of constitutions adopted at the time of independence. The idea that government must adhere to the rule of law in ways that uphold the fundamental individual and collective rights of all citizens has not been heeded by post-colonial states. Constitutional instruments have also failed to effectively hold governments accountable to the principle of constitutionalism. Whatever the precise reasons may have been from country to country - and they are no doubt complex and often controversial - the fact remains that the principle of constitutionalism is weak in most African countries. Almost all of the first constitutions were either suspended or radically altered by military usurpers or single-party states within a few years of independence. Regardless of the explanations that one may suggest or subscribe to, it seems clear that local populations were unwilling or unable to resist the erosion or manipulation of their national constitutions and governments by civilian and military leaders alike.

The weakness of the principle of constitutionalism in post-colonial African states and the failure of their constitutions are part of the wider problem of the lack of a dynamic relationship between civil society and state institutions and processes. Part of the root cause of this problem, it seems to me, is the fact that the present nation state was an externally imposed concept, rather than an indigenous growth evolving out of the lived experiences and cultural values of African societies. African societies appear to regard the post-colonial state with profound mistrust and have no sense of ownership of it nor expectation of protection or service from it. They tend to tolerate its existence as an unavoidable evil, but prefer to have as little interaction with its institutions and processes as possible.

One contribution that follow-up activities from the present project might make is to construct a tentative and coherent model for understanding and documenting the nature and causes of the negative relationship between civil society and the state in each country, without

---

12 Constitutionalism refers to a cluster of norms, institutions and processes pertaining to the rule of law, political participation, protection of fundamental rights, and so forth. But the concept should also be seen as dynamic and adaptable to different contexts.

claiming to do so definitively or exhaustively. Other subsequent activities can attempt to develop strategies for overcoming the sense of apathy and powerlessness among the people at large toward the state and its institutions, including the constitutional and legal order. The legal protection of human rights is both a goal in itself and part of the means for reaching this goal in Africa. It is important to acknowledge both the reality and the negative consequences of the present relationship between civil society and the state and its implications for the principle of constitutionalism. Otherwise, it would be merely wishful thinking, if not actually harmful, to speak of the legal protection of human rights under African constitutions.

In summary, the features of the majority of post-colonial states in Africa are relevant for the purposes of our project. These states are the product of arbitrary colonial histories and decolonisation processes, continuing the same authoritarian policies and exceeding them in their ability to oppress and control, rather than protect and serve their citizens. They are based on ad hoc constitutional systems which were hurriedly set up at independence, only to collapse or be emptied of all meaningful content within a few years. Their legal systems are usually poor copies of the colonial legal systems, lacking legitimacy and relevance to the lives of the majority of the population at large. Many African states also suffer from cycles of alternating civilian and military rule that disrupt the stability and continuity needed to build traditions and institutions of government and enable the rule of law to take root and grow. Their economies are weak and dependent on global processes beyond their control.

It seems clear to me that much of what I have said in this chapter is supported by the findings and analysis of the country studies which are presented thematically in Chapter 3. However, it is important to emphasise that the purpose of that synthesis is not simply to present an accurate picture of the current status of legal protection of human rights under African constitutions. Rather, the objective is to provide a realistic basis for developing strategies to transform the present reality in favour of greater and more effective protection for human rights, using the means and processes provided by the legal system. This goal is based on the firm conviction that state practice can be changed in this way, provided that appropriate strategies are put in place, and it is grounded in a firm belief in the ability of African peoples to protect their own human rights.

Chapter 2

Human Rights, Development and Globalisation: Reflections on Agendas and Challenges for Africa[1]

Shirin Aumeeruddy-Cziffra

Ladies and gentlemen, dear friends.

First of all I must thank the organisers for calling upon me to deliver the keynote speech on this extremely important occasion. I am so glad to be here amongst friends, most of whom I have known as militants engaged in the struggle in favour of Human Rights for several years.

Moreover, I cannot hide my delight at being in Dakar, where not only do I have good memories, but as all Mauritians I feel particularly touched as some of my compatriots are of Senegalese descent. Even though the historical conditions which led to their emigration to such far-away lands is no matter of pride, and even if it is impossible today to trace back our origins individually, I wish to place on record my country's sentimental attachment to Africa through the origins of its people from Senegal, Mozambique, and Madagascar.

Friends, our conference calls us to look at 'The Legal Protection of Human Rights under the Constitutions of Africa' but I am sure that there is consensus that we must also briefly analyse the historical, sociological, cultural and other causes of non-respect of freedom and liberty on our Continent in order to grasp the profound reasons that have given rise to such practices. It is only by this broader approach that we can start thinking of legal solutions, on the premise that everyone here is conscious of the limitations of law by itself. I believe that we are all on the same wavelength. The legal protection of rights, however we may define them, can only be meaningful if it is part of a comprehensive strategy to reinforce democracy and development. I understand that some of you will be sharing your analysis on the specificity of certain countries later on and that my role today is to open up the debate on as wide a spectrum as possible.

I shall therefore draw from my varied experience in local and international politics, and try to analyse the role of Africa and Africans in

---

1   This paper was delivered as the keynote speech to the Dakar Conference in the author's absence due to ill health.

the perspective of this new millennium by looking firstly at the issues at stake from a geopolitical standpoint, by assessing the challenges we have to face, more specially in this new era, where globalization is the order of the day. No State can afford to remain isolated and ignore international developments. I will therefore, as we go along, identify the kinds of action that we can take either on our own or by joining efforts with others. This means looking at what others are doing or can do and discussing who are those we could really work with, as well as the specific components of our own contribution, be it in terms of action in the field of law or any other global way.

The international media have unfortunately too often projected a negative image of Africa and invented the term 'afro-pessimism'. True it is that our continent is still very much in turmoil, most countries are finding it very difficult to attain high standards of development. But at the same time some countries and some regions are doing so well now that they are attracting newcomers from everywhere. It is in this context that we would be best advised to study different cases and think of specific approaches whilst also comparing with a view to finding ways of co-operating between ourselves.

In any case, this is not the time to cry over spilt milk but rather to imagine new ways of making the most of what we have. In this context, it is important to remember that African unity is essential if not only from a moral point of view, at least because of the absolute necessity to share our expertise and know-how and create strong regional organisations. If this is true of governmental strategies, it is also relevant for non-governmental action. We now know how to network and this is precisely what we are doing in this conference organised by several networks. Let us say that improving our networks is one of our priorities.

In the post-GATT (General Agreement of Trades and Tariffs) era, regionalization is a must and it is normal for all countries to make alliances that will benefit their own economies and allow them to be competitive on the world market. In fact economic factors dictate our policies to such an extent that the sovereignty of modern States is now a totally different concept. In colonial days, we knew who our masters were even if we had not chosen them. Later on, we sometimes knew who our friends were. Nowadays we are told that the world is a global village and that we all depend on one another. At Marrakech,[2] many countries of the South were

---

2   The city in Morocco where the treaty was signed.

mere spectators but still had to accept the World Trade Organization (WTO) and its diktats. That does not necessarily mean that we have no say in our own countries any more but we must adapt to the new world environment. In so doing, we need not sacrifice our values and adopt exogenous solutions that have no relevance whatsoever in our countries, but we would be wise to examine whatever obtains elsewhere in any field and choose with wisdom those avenues that seem more appropriate. This sounds so simple and yet do we not know how strategic mistakes in the past have had negative impacts on our development process. Of course lawyers, scholars and grassroots workers—nay, the people—have little say in such matters in most African countries. Indeed, populations who live in rural areas usually have to accept decisions taken by a minority from the urban zones even though they may be the main suppliers of agricultural produce. The quality of participation of the people, and that of different groups, for example women, minorities, youth and even the older generation, the disabled etc., is an essential part of democracy and development. The proper way to ensure the full participation and protection of all vulnerable groups is an important question that we have to address. In most constitutions, there is a non-discrimination section which purports to afford equal treatment to all citizens but we know that there are often categories that are missing either on purpose or through sheer unawareness. But it is also necessary sometimes to provide for positive discrimination for such persons.

What can be our contribution in our respective countries or regions? How do we strengthen our own organisations? How do we empower our own people so that they may participate fully in decision-making and have some kind of contribution in the shaping of their destiny? How do we relate to each other, to our governments, to organisations abroad having similar objectives and to regional entities like the Southern African Development Community (SADC), the Common Market of Eastern and Southern Africa, the Economic Community of West African States (ECOWAS), the Indian Ocean Commission etc.? And of course, what is our role within the Organisation of African Unity (OAU)?

It is naturally in the latter that we have placed our hopes, and it is proper that we should have struggled in order to be able to express ourselves before its Commission for Human and Peoples' Rights. Many organisations represented here today already have an observer status with the Commission. Admittedly, its mode of functioning is not perfect but we must keep on struggling and try to impact on decisions at that level and not seek merely to obtain the right of speech, just to express our frustrations. This is one area which I feel we could explore during this conference. We know, for example, that it is possible to present proposals to the Commission which will eventually get on the agenda of Heads of State and Government. If we also manage to lobby our respective representatives, they can in turn prove to be efficient allies in the proper forums. Advocacy and lobbying are our most effective tools.

At present two questions are being ushered before the Commission: the creation of an African Court on Human and Peoples' Rights, and hopefully the adoption of an Optional Protocol on Women's Rights to give African States the means to respect their international commitments taken by adopting the Beijing Platform of Action in 1995. Without the input of NGOs such questions have no chance of being discussed.

As regards the OAU, we can hardly remain silent about its limited means and ability to act. On the other hand, there is a risk that new emerging regional organisations will attract so much attention that they may forget the rest of Africa. Even in Mauritius when we hear politicians speak of the SADC, of which we are a member, we make a point of reminding them that we are part of a whole continent which desperately needs the help of its more fortunate regions.

If we feel that we can also act on an international basis, then we must identify those forums where our efforts will have direct or indirect bearing on issues that will be affecting us at home. To take an example of a matter which is dear to my heart, the gender issue, it is obvious that we have won several battles because of the perseverance of women's organisations from all over the world. Perhaps the younger generations do not remember how women literally hijacked the first World Conference on Women in Mexico in 1975. In fact NGOs' participation was not recognised in those days and they made history by imposing the setting up of an NGO Forum parallel to the official conference which only government representatives could attend. And the kind of pressure that has been maintained for the past two decades on the women's front, which has now gained the active support of all human rights lovers, is an excellent proof that solidarity is essential and can work wonders. Since 1975, the United Nations Organisation has agreed to organise NGO forums each time a question touching on basic rights is to be discussed. And we all know what has been the influence of the participation of NGOs in the Conference on Human Rights in Vienna in 1993 where African NGOs played an important role in the debate which resulted in the recognition of the Right to Development being as important as Civil and Political Rights.

In fact in countries where there is a will to show that democracy is scrupulous, governments even consult specialised organisations and sometimes include a few representatives of the civil society in their official delegations, which may give rise to controversy if NGOs do not federate their energies and have their own mode of selection. In some cases country reports for such occasions or those that have to be submitted to specialised UN committees created by some Treaties are also prepared with the help of local organisations which are in contact with international organisations acting as watchdogs and could damage a country's public image. As we can see, in countries where democracy flourishes, there is a wide scope of action for advocates who can use the sophisticated methods of pressure that exist both nationally and abroad. In relevant regions we may also consider being part of a pressure group and organise awareness campaigns to obtain change of policy on any matter which involves human rights. We can think of numerous ways of acting in such countries. More and more now, lawyers, who are also militating for change, can even convince their governments to let them or their organisation prepare draft legislation. Most governments cannot afford to get any serious legislative work done for lack of competent drafters even if policy decisions have been taken. And let us not forget that if specific laws do not provide for the protection of specific rights, most of those that are beautifully spelt out in a Constitution will prove useless.

Further, it is important to see how far international norms are included in our law and are protected by our Constitutions. As lawyers know, in some countries the mere ratification of an international instrument is not *per se* applicable internally. This is the case, I believe, in all Commonwealth countries including Mauritius. It is very rare at home to have the National Assembly adopt a Treaty *in toto*.

But we can certainly lobby for amendments to be brought to existing laws or the preparation of new legislation if need be. In my country, we started campaigning for the amendment of the Civil Code in the 1970s and family law giving women equal rights then changed drastically. But it took us 20 years to remove gender discrimination from the Constitution. Our campaign in the 1970s federated women from all walks of life, it cut across party allegiance, because it touched on issues which were concrete like property rights, right to get one's own salary, rights over children and no woman felt unconcerned. However when we spoke of the Constitution somehow it looked less urgent. In fact few people understand the value of constitutional law. Further, unless there are strong Courts to give effect to the rights which are therein contained, protection is purely theoretical.

Let me give you another example. On the question of the abolition of the death penalty our government finally gave in, but it has not been removed completely from our Constitution, and our present Attorney General has said publicly that he is in favour of reintroducing this barbarous and inefficient sentence for cases of drug trafficking. You will certainly be interested to know that when the Dangerous Drugs Act was first amended to introduce the death penalty, six members of the Opposition obtained the right to vote according to conscience and not toe the party line. This kind of refinement is possible only in countries where there is a democratically elected Parliament. This of course has not always been the case in Mauritius. Perhaps at this stage you would like to hear about our experience, which cannot be transplanted elsewhere but may throw some light on the subject.

Today Mauritius is considered to be amongst those countries which have the best human rights record. But compatriots of my generation still remember the dark days when we lived under a state of emergency, elections were postponed, press censorship was our daily lot, trade unionists were imprisoned and all fundamental freedoms were suspended. Of course we had only just become independent and we had a brand new Constitution on the same model as all ex-British colonies. Its second chapter protects fundamental rights and freedoms of the individual but there can be derogation from these during any period of public emergency which means not just wartime, but also when 'there is in force a resolution of the Assembly declaring that democratic institutions are threatened by subversion' or that the measures 'are required in the interest of peace, order and good government.' These provisions are considered normal since there are always limitations to the exercise of any right in order to protect the rights of others and of the community as a whole. But they must be used judiciously and not just to stifle political opponents.

When elections took place in 1967, the issue at stake was the independence of the country and the Alliance led by Sir Seewoosagur

Ramgoolam, our present Prime Minister's father, proposing to break away from Great Britain won against the then opposition, led by Sir Ga'tan Duval, which nevertheless secured 44 per cent of the votes. However, the latter, instead of playing fully his role of watchdog as Leader of the Opposition at the National Assembly, decided to join the Government which thus had an absolute majority and could therefore amend the section of the Constitution which requires an exceptional 75 per cent majority to postpone General Elections, abolish Municipal Elections and By Elections. That is why we could not exercise our right of vote for nine years—the normal mandate being five years. The State of Emergency was maintained until 1976 when General Elections were finally organised.

What did we do? We resisted and used every means at our disposal to mobilise the people even though public gatherings were forbidden. I think that, despite the suspension of elections, if the new regime had governed the country in the interests of the people, perhaps they would have stayed in power much longer. After all not far from us in Seychelles, where President Albert René came to power by a coup and where there were no elections for a much longer period, when he did organise multipartite elections, and allowed ex-President Mancham to come back from exile and contest these elections, the latter lost and René was elected with flying colours. His case is quite interesting because it seems to destroy all theories about parliamentary democracy being the best form of government, and to prove that a benevolent despot can help to get a country back on the right track. But that was in a special context, and rested too much on one person's commitment. We are concerned with institutions and not individuals. This is why rights have to be guaranteed by law, and preferably by the supreme law which has precedence over all others and cannot be amended by a simple majority.

To come back to the example of Mauritius, after Independence, the socio-economic situation went from bad to worse. Twenty per cent of the active population was unemployed, salaries were frozen but the prices of basic commodities kept going up. At that time, a new opposition party lead by Paul Berenger was born to fill the gap left by Duval's party. Despite repression, its activists managed to reorganise the trade unions, and the situation was so bad that each time one of its leaders was imprisoned, a new one emerged. It was when M. Berenger was detained for a whole year that lawyers came to assist him and were won to his cause. Of these the most famous was Aneerood Jugnauth who later served as Prime Minister for 13 years. Berenger himself has since then occupied several key positions and is at present Leader of the Opposition.

The Mauritian contemporary history is very interesting, but we will not be able to go in much greater detail, our objective being merely to draw a few lessons. First I wish to comment on so called governments of national unity. I have always been amazed that in many African countries, when a government is being formed, all parties want to join in. I know that sometimes it is in the spirit of national reconciliation but to my mind, it is so important to have a strong opposition that I am hard to convince on that score. Perhaps I am too westernised and have difficulty to appreciate the importance of consensus building, which is not only an African value but also a very Asian one. But in my 15 years as a Member of Parliament, out of which 12 were spent in the Opposition, I honestly believe that, when parliamentary democracy works well, opposition MPs can have as positive an impact as those in Government. In the Westminster type of parliament which we have, members can contribute quite seriously to national debates, they can make important suggestions, propose amendments to laws, and consensus can be reached on various matters. But the role which I find essential from the point of view of human rights is that of being able to question each minister on his actions or omissions. This forces government to be transparent.

The very principle of modern democracy is that all elected persons are accountable to the people because they only act by virtue of a mandate, is it not?

My other comments regarding the experience we had can be summarised as follows: the period of emergency could not have lasted long because we already had strong democratic institutions and more specially an independent judiciary and a strong press. Further our people are educated. We have recourse to the Supreme Court as often as need be. Right now I am the leading counsel in a constitutional case against Government contesting its right to create a Privatisation Fund which is not part of the Consolidated Fund, which means that it is not part of the normal budgetary exercise. In other words it reduces the role of elected members and increases the power of the Executive.

As you may also know, when our Constitution did not provide us with a remedy, we have in the past sent a communication to the UN Human

Rights Committee. The point is that I was able, as a mere citizen, to contest laws adopted locally before an international body, the reason being that my government had not only ratified the Covenant on Civil and Political Rights but had also ratified the Optional Protocol which allows a citizen to enter a communication against his own country. Mauritius was at the time one of the rare countries to have ratified the Optional Protocol. That shows a will to submit a country's action to international scrutiny, which indeed constitutes a high degree of respect for human rights. Unfortunately since the law was not amended despite the conclusions of The Human Rights Committee given in April 1981, that respect looked very much like lip service. The irony of History is that, a year later, I became Attorney General and amended the laws myself. You will also like to know that one of the first amendments we brought to the Constitution was to restore to the people their right of vote fully, that is to restore all elections and make it impossible to postpone any General Elections except with a unanimous vote and a referendum.

These points, I believe, are central to our conference. What can people do if their fundamental rights are infringed? Even when those rights are guaranteed by the Constitution, how does one obtain protection? What happens if a Constitution does not enshrine what we consider to be a fundamental right? What can we do if there is no real Constitution? What protection can people expect if there is no State but just a semblance of an organisation? Even worse still what can we do from outside if the people are either too ignorant or too poor or too powerless to react? These are a few questions that we must put and possibly try to answer. I know that originally the Conference was to target only those new emerging democratic nations. But it was wise to open up the discussion since we know how fragile most of the new democracies are and how conflicts in one country can spread like fire in a whole region.

I am a great believer in concerted action. If we want to be able to have an impact on the destiny of our countries or even on our continent, we must try and fit in our proper place on the world scene. To come back to what I said earlier on, we must organise ourselves in order to have a multi-disciplinary action. We are lawyers. We believe that the rule of law is essential. But what are we prepared to do to bring about the rule of law in countries where there is complete chaos?

I want to emphasise the duty which is ours to help and empower those who are already engaged in bringing radical changes to development policies in their countries. Many funders will sponsor all actions likely to promote sustainable development. That includes attempts to fight against corruption, wastage, mismanagement, economic crimes and of course all forms of human rights abuse.

In international diplomacy the term used is 'good governance'. It may sound like a concept of the Western world designed to penalise countries from the South. Indeed some of our people feel sour at the sometimes inhuman attitude of bilateral and multilateral donors, when they threaten to cut aid unless there is a strong commitment on the part of governments to curtail unnecessary expenses, to fight efficiently against corruption and to readjust the economy. Unfortunately it is the masses that suffer when these measures are too drastic. Often the people are paying for the extravagant way of life of those in power and also, let us be frank, because some dictators have had external support in order to seize and/or remain in power. In that context it is sometimes also useful to alert public opinion in those countries where people in power are giving support to dictators in our homeland.

In Mauritius, we also went through the ordeal of structural adjustment in 1982. We had to close some secondary schools and it was impossible to grant the percentage of salary compensation which we would have liked to have given. But since we decided to reduce our own MP and ministers' allowances and voluntarily refused to benefit from all duty-free privileges attached to our posts, there was no crisis and the people agreed to sacrifice for a few more years.

This goes to show that when there is a need for structural adjustment, the burden must be shared by one and all. Can lawyers remain quiet when the people are unjustly bearing the brunt of these programmes and those in power continue to lead lavish lives at public expense? This concerns social and economic rights and may, for all we know, be guaranteed by the Constitution. It may be the opportunity for a test case or direct local or international lobbying. We can approach indirectly the World Bank and/or the International Monetary Fund (IMF) to seek either a review of the programme or better monitoring. International allies are very important in such cases. But at all times we must beware of those in power who resist any form of readjustment and pretend that they only have the people's interests at heart.

Also we must never fall in the trap of those who put forward the defence of tradition to rationalise their unwillingness to respect human rights on the grounds that they were invented by western powers to control us better. There is a lot to be said about human rights abuse in Europe and in the United States and about the double language of some political leaders who do not practise what they preach. That does not entitle anyone to use these as an excuse to penalise their own people who have inherent inalienable and indivisible rights as human beings. The right to life and security was not invented by anyone. The right to hold opinions, to speak freely and to be heard are natural rights which should be enjoyed by one and all. But they had to be formally drafted and translated in international instruments that would become norms for everyone. Nowadays we can say that only positive traditions are acceptable. The most difficult is refusal on religious grounds. We cannot deal with this otherwise than by making sure that people are educated and develop their own critical mind in order to make the right choices. I think it is obvious that the type of resistance we are talking about can only succeed in countries where the people are living in appalling conditions. This brings us back to the question of development.

We now have to find ways and means to get our continent to take off and not remain on the roadside, while others discover the riches we possess not only in terms of natural resources, but also as a human resource pool and as a market. Democracy and development are interdependent and, though there are attempts to place them in a specific order of hierarchy, we must refuse this attitude which, even when it is innocent, can place our countries in a situation which very much resembles a vicious circle. There is no democracy without development, but can there be development without democracy? In some Asian countries, as we all know, they would have us believe that democracy is a luxury only people from the North can afford, and that their economies are booming. But who benefits from the wealth that has indeed been created? It is accepted now that development must be human-centred if it is to have any meaning at all. In order to ensure this, there must be the rule of law and strong democratic institutions to safeguard fundamental rights.

Unfortunately on our continent, despite progress achieved in several countries, there are still too many regions where the most fundamental human rights are trampled upon daily and where populations are still living in absolute terror and in the most destitute conditions. There are too many countries where the risks of armed conflict are still very high. During this last decade, the international community started putting pressure for the democratisation of the whole continent. Indeed we sometimes had the feeling that there was too much rush to force some countries, that were not yet ready, to hold multiparty elections. For what is the use of elections if the people do not fully understand what they stand for, who's who and what real changes will be brought about? We all know that the electoral process is very complex and it is now current practice to obtain aid from the UN, the OAU and other multilateral sources like the Commonwealth and the Francophonie not only to send observers at election time, but specially to prepare those consultations long in advance both from a material standpoint and in terms of awareness campaigns. They can also be important forums for us, as we can not only benefit from aid for specific programmes but look for support from strong member States in other fora, for example, the European Union. At the recent African, Caribbean and Pacific Countries Summit in Libreville, such support was precious. Both these organisations have opened up an avenue which has great value for the poorer States whose debts have been erased by France and Britain respectively at recent meetings.

Further both organisations also have specific programmes to enlarge democracy: these include law reform, codification, training of lawyers, of magistrates, of judicial officers, of policemen, data collection, computerisation of jurisprudence, gender awareness, children's rights etc. And all these programmes are carried out by consultants from member States in collaboration with local experts. It is in the particular situation when a country is preparing for change that we could play a meaningful role. It is the natural mission of NGOs to engage in promoting a human rights culture and imagine the best tools that will reach the people even in the most isolated areas.

In countries where it is possible to communicate to the masses without facing repression, this kind of action must be ongoing. In those where the regime is already in the public international eye, it will certainly be facilitated. But we should beware as the excitement that usually prevails at pre-election time renders our task difficult. Lots of people want to intervene in such times, some genuinely, others for selfish reasons and it is important to be able to identify all those who are already engaged, to design efficient programmes in the right places at the right times. Fortunately when international and regional organisations are involved, there is every chance that there will be co-ordinated action and experts from African countries are called upon to play an important role.

In those times it is important to make sure that everyone has an identity under Civil Status laws and that the laws relating to elections are properly drafted and provide for free and fair elections and for an acceptable mechanism to organise and supervise the popular consultation. In many countries, the electoral system is described in the Constitution which provides all guarantees. Ideally before one reaches that stage, there is a Constitutional Conference and lawyers and activists can certainly play a key role in reaching a consensus. Later it will be important to engage, either directly or through local groups, in the proper registration of electors.

NGOs that are organised regionally can concentrate on capacity building to prepare others to act efficiently in numerous situations which demand a great mobilisation of the masses. In this context, we must never forget that there is a price to pay for democracy including the mere cost of setting up any worthwhile project. We depend a lot on aid from donors and luckily there are some funds that are available for good programmes. But we all know that the task is so huge and the funds so rare, that we must also bear in mind that we should plan ahead even in terms of fund-raising including from local sources. In those regions where the private sector is fully engaged in the development process, we can always convince firms to donate in favour of serious actions that will ensure peace, security and social stability which are essential ingredients to their prosperity and that of the nation as a whole. Further, we all realise that, even if we have friends outside, it is high time for Africans themselves to be in the forefront of the struggle for a real democratisation process throughout the continent. It is indeed a matter of survival for us. We have no choice. Besides, although it would be vain to indulge in passé attitudes about the evils of colonisation, we must still remain vigilant as new masters are often lurking in difficult times and may pose as saviours. Indeed changes of leadership, but not necessarily of regime, are still taking place by armed forces and the international community seems quite powerless expressing only its hope that elections will eventually take place.

We are not fire-fighters. We cannot run all over the place trying to solve crises. But if we mean business, there is a lot we can do in a long term perspective. If we are credible our voices will be heard specially if we all join forces. The task is huge. Most of you here have been very active for years and you know all the challenges that we have to face. My task was only to underline them and open several avenues of debate. I have done and will now look forward to listening to you all. Thank you for bearing with me.

Chapter 3

Protecting Human Rights in Plural Legal Systems of Africa: A Comparative Overview

Abdullahi A. An-Na'im

As noted in Chapter 1, a major component of this project was the preparation of country studies examining the protection for human rights under African legal systems in specific African countries. Two broad and unifying guidelines governed preparation of the country studies, as well as the project as a whole. First, the ultimate objective of the project is to enhance and promote the *legal protection of human rights* under the constitution (or existing constitutional order, where there is no constitution as such in force in the country). As indicated in the report of the Planning Meeting for the project, the Lusaka Report,[1] the concept of legal protection refers to the 'total process of deploying the law for the purpose of vindicating human rights'.[2] It must be emphasised, however, that taking this focus as the agreed mandate and field of professional competence of the authors of country studies does not mean that the legal process is the only, or even the primary, way of protecting human rights. Nor does this focus mean that this subject can or should be studied in isolation from other approaches in a broader local, regional or global context. Second, the country studies are intended to serve as the *basis of a multi-faceted strategy*, which will ultimately include litigation, information exchange, training and legislative advocacy, as discussed in other parts of this book.

The Lusaka Report highlighted broad, general characteristics of the legal framework for the protection of human rights in many African jurisdictions. It was therefore intended as a source of general guidance rather than a detailed blueprint for the more specific and detailed country studies that would follow.[3] The more specific guidelines issued to the authors for the content of their reports emphasised the importance of structural and organisational consistency and comprehensive coverage of the issues, in order to develop valid general conclusions, make appropriate policy recommendations, and propose practical strategies for systematic

---

1 *The Legal Protection of Human Rights Under the Constitutions of Africa: Report of Planning Meeting, Lusaka, Zambia, 28-30 July 1995*, prepared by Chidi Anselm Odinkalu, available from INTERIGHTS.

2 Ibid. p. 20.

3 Id.

action to protect human rights under African legal systems. The authors were asked to organise their country studies under six headings: Introduction; Constitutional and Legal Framework for the Protection of Human Rights; the Judiciary and the Legal Profession; Political, Social and Economic Context; Status and Role of Non-Governmental Organisations; and Conclusions and Recommendations. In their introductions the authors were asked to give an overview of the historical background and demographic profile of the country. In the conclusions, they were to provide an integrated and coherent evaluation of the current status and future prospects for the legal protection of human rights in the country studied. They were also asked to make practical and concrete policy recommendations, taking into account the realities described in the preceding sections.

Although the authors had clear guidelines to follow, there was considerable scope for individualised interpretation of the guidelines because each country's legal system is the product of its history, traditions and current realities. Not all the commissioned studies were received in time for inclusion in the synthesis prepared for the Dakar Conference, or this updated revised version of it, and some of the studies received did not address all the suggested topics. From those studies received, one can see some clear patterns, themes and similarities which are highlighted in the subsequent sections of this summary. As will be seen in the forthcoming book which will include as many of the country studies as we eventually receive and can edit for publication, the great value of those studies lies in their wealth and specificity of detail, the overview they provide of the legal framework for human rights protections in the countries studied, and the political, economic, social and civil society context in which the legal systems function. These studies collect in one place, often for the first time, detailed information about the dimensions of the protection for human rights provided through the legal system in a cross-section of African countries.

Since some of the commissioned countries studies were not received in time for inclusion in this synthesis, and some of those received did not closely follow the suggested guidelines, the following synthesis cannot claim to be comprehensive or exhaustive of the situation even in those countries identified for study by the Lusaka Planning Meeting.[4] Information and analysis presented in the four core descriptive sections of the country studies received may be synthesised as follows.

---

4 See the Introduction, *supra*, for the criteria of selection. The countries selected by the Lusaka Meeting and authors were Botswana (Rahim Khan), Egypt (Amir Salem), Ethiopia (Meaza Ashenafi, Yosias Tadesse), Ghana & Togo (Nana K. A. Busia Jr.), Guinea (Amadou Sakho, Ibrahima Kane), Kenya (Katurima M'Inoti, Mwangi Mbuthia), Morocco (Abdelaziz Nouaydi), Mozambique (Luis Mondlane, Gita Honwana Welch), Nigeria (Olisa Agbakoba), Rwanda (Bibiane Mbaye Gahamanyi), Senegal (Abdoullah Cisse), South Africa (Lucrecia Seafield), Sudan (Siddig A. Hussein), Uganda (Livingstone Sewanyana), Zambia (Michelo Hunsungule). The study on Nigeria was conducted before the recent transition to civil rule in that country.

Constitutional and Legal Framework for the Protection of Human Rights

In this section, authors were asked to explain the *normative framework* of the legal protection of human rights through an examination of the origins, main developments and current status of the constitutional and legal system in their respective country, followed by an overview of constitutional provisions relating to the protection of human rights. This section was to address all aspects and possibilities of the formal legal view of the protection of rights: what the law says *should* happen. The relationship between the theory and actual practice would then emerge in subsequent sections of the study. Authors were urged to discuss the status and role, if any, of customary (including religious) law and practice, and its relationship to the so-called 'state' or 'statutory' legal system of the country. They were also asked to assess whether customary law and practice are subject to an overriding concern with the protection of constitutional and/or human rights.

African countries may be characterised or classified in different ways, but, for the purposes of this report, it might be useful to consider them in terms of whether the government is, on the whole, an aid or an obstacle to the legal protection of human rights. Whether a country's legal system is based on common or civil law is not the most important factor in determining its stance toward the legal protection of human rights. Similarly, whether a country has a federal system, like Nigeria, or a unitary system, like Mozambique and Zambia, is immaterial in principle for the protection of human rights, although the constitutional framework and institutional arrangements under each type of system will probably vary significantly. There was a clear consensus in the reports that a democratic system protects human rights better than does a military or other authoritarian system. Not every study specifically addressed this question, but those that did agreed on this view. Some authors sought to show how repressive governments are able to shape the law to their own advantage, so that the law itself is used as a means to violate widely accepted human rights norms. For example, KANU (Kenya African National Union), which has had almost exclusive control of the government of Kenya since independence, has constitutionalised political conditions favourable to itself and consolidated legal powers in the executive branch.

Although the studies received did provide some bases for classification of governments in terms of their commitment to the protection of human rights under their national legal systems, advocates should neither assume that a good record will necessarily be kept, nor abandon the effort with governments which have a bad record. Rather, the point is that a realistic understanding of the practice of one government or another is relevant to strategic and tactical decisions about practical approaches to be adopted in each case. It is also important to note that even governments which may be considered 'friendly' to human rights concerns may face serious difficulties in protecting and promoting them, for a variety of reasons, including the country's history and traditions, resource constraints, and external or internal pressures.

Constitutions

The constitutions of most African countries still closely resemble in form and content the Western constitutional forms they inherited. For example, most constitutions of former British colonies establish similar governmental structures: subject to the rule of law; composed of executive, legislative and judicial branches; and incorporating some form of a bill of rights. Their content and theoretical orientation clearly reflect the influence of the British and U.S. systems of government and the European Enlightenment ethos in general, for example, in the notions of separation of powers, individual liberties and due process protections. Evidence of the influence of Western constitutional theory and history can be seen in the recognition given to civil and political rights in most African constitutions. Even repressive governments give lip service to these notions, although many have created mechanisms within their legal system for circumventing in practice the constitutional guarantees.

There is widespread constitutional protection for freedom of speech, religion and assembly. Trade and labour union rights are often included as well. Most of the constitutions include a provision respecting the right to life, although they do permit an exception for capital punishment. South Africa is an exception; in 1995 the Constitutional Court of South Africa declared the death penalty unconstitutional, in a decision that went contrary to public opinion (South Africa, 43).[5]

The constitutions of African countries also provide for due process protections, such as *habeas corpus* and the right to a fair trial for the

---

5 Page references in this synthesis are to the text of the draft studies kept on file at the offices of INTERIGHTS in London.

criminally accused. Most of the constitutions prohibit discrimination on grounds of sex, religion, race or ethnicity and so forth, although the application of such clauses with respect to women may be limited in some countries. For example, in Morocco, the non-discrimination provision in the constitution guarantees women's equality with respect to political rights only (Morocco, 10-11).

None of the countries surveyed provide full-fledged constitutional protection for economic, social and cultural (ESC) rights. It is worth noting that in not providing constitutional protection for these rights, they are consistent with the vast majority of countries in the world. Some constitutions, however, among them those of Namibia and Uganda, include some of these rights under headings such as 'Directive Principles of State Policy' (see, e.g., Uganda, 6). In addition, the Ugandan constitution includes the right to education and to a clean and healthy environment within its chapter on Fundamental Rights and Freedoms (Uganda, 8). This chapter also includes provisions permitting public interest litigation, by broadening the traditional rules of standing to allow individuals and groups to sue on behalf of the human rights of others (Uganda, 8). The 1996 South African constitution also gives third parties standing to sue on behalf of others in cases of threatened or actual infringement of a right or to bring public interest lawsuits (South Africa, 16).

South Africa is in the vanguard world-wide in providing constitutional protection for certain ESC rights, including the rights to access to adequate housing, health care, food, water, social security, and basic education, as well as some specific children's rights (South Africa, 12). As is true of the International Covenant on Economic, Social and Cultural Rights, economic and social rights in the South African constitution are subject to progressive realisation. Constitutional and statutory schemes, although superficially similar in different countries, may be realised in very different ways, depending on the extent to which the government is open and accessible through legal accountability to its citizens. Most African countries have a written constitution, but many of these constitutions have been (or are currently) totally or partially 'suspended' for considerable periods of time, or drastically 'amended' in an extra-legal manner, if not totally abrogated by a military coup d'état or other revolutionary regime. Major changes or complete replacement of the constitution at the behest of the executive branch serve to demonstrate its dominance over the legal system and the lack of true separation of powers. The constitution of Nigeria has been partially suspended so drastically and for such a long period of time (Nigeria, 15) that it is probably misleading to say that the country has a constitution at all. Sudan has had three transitional constitutions in the forty years since independence, in 1956, 1964 and 1985, marking its periods of civilian rule. Since the military coup d'état in 1989, it has been ruled under a series of authoritarian decrees (Sudan, 6-11, 14-18). Rwanda has had four constitutions since independence, including the current constitutional framework, known as the fundamental law, which has been in force since 1995 (Rwanda, 4-6). A new constitution does not have to represent a step backwards. In Uganda and South Africa, the constitutions of 1995 and 1996, respectively, represent significant progress over their predecessors in terms of protection for human rights and popular participation in their drafting.

International Human Rights Agreements

Most of the countries studied have ratified the major international human rights agreements, including the African Charter on Human and Peoples' Rights. In general, these agreements have been ratified without major reservations. Perhaps the most notable exception among the countries surveyed is Morocco's reservations to CEDAW, the Convention on the Elimination of All Forms of Discrimination Against Women. Morocco has ratified CEDAW to the extent that it does not conflict with *Shari'a*, particularly the law of personal status, and the traditional rights and responsibilities in marriage, reservations that are common among predominantly Islamic countries. Morocco does not endorse the right of a woman to choose her domicile or to transmit her nationality to her children of a foreign father (Morocco, 10-11).

Legal Systems

Like their constitutions, the legal systems described in the country studies appear to be broadly based on Western models, of either the common law or civil law variety. The choice of one system or another is a product of colonial experience, and is not itself indicative of whether or to what extent human rights are legally protected in the country.

For ordinary people, the imported legal systems are likely to be alien, intimidating, inaccessible, and prohibitively expensive. Courts are usually located in the larger towns and cities, often far removed from rural areas. Perceptions concerning the inaccessibility and alienation of a 'foreign' system are only exacerbated when courtroom proceedings are conducted in European languages that the parties do not understand (Rwanda, 18; Uganda, 24-25). The result is particularly anomalous when all the major actors in the courtroom - judge or magistrate, attorneys, parties - speak the same local language as their first language, yet the proceedings are still conducted in the foreign language (South Africa, 52-53).

In view of the colonial origin and continued 'dependency' of most African legal systems, it is interesting to note that almost all country studies took the basic tenets of these legal systems for granted. For many of the authors, it appears that the chief difficulty is not the statutes themselves or the foreign origin of much of the legal system, but rather problems of implementation and the constraints of resource limitations.

Some of the studies mention efforts to fashion a legal system more truly responsive to an African context. A good example is the 'Popular Justice' system in force in Mozambique from 1975-1992. As described in the Mozambique report, this system appeared to be a response to the alienation and inadequacy of the colonial legal system. However, since 1992, changes to major features of the Popular Justice system have returned the Mozambican legal system to a more traditional model.

Legal Mechanisms for the Limitation of Human Rights
Despite the existence of human rights protections in most African constitutions, repressive governments have found numerous ways to limit or eliminate protection on a theoretical level, as well as in practice. The most important of these 'constitutional' limitations and restrictions can be outlined as follows:

States of Emergency
States of emergency appear to be the norm, rather than the exception, in several African countries, and the criteria and procedures for regulating them generally grant considerable discretion to the executive branch of government. For example, Zambia was under a state of emergency for most of the period from July 1964 (two months before independence) until 1991. Sudan has been under a state of emergency since 1989. Nigeria is living under a *de facto* state of emergency (Nigeria, 26). In contrast, the

constitution of Botswana permits derogation from fundamental rights and freedoms in cases of war or public emergency, but in the thirty years since independence, this power has never been invoked (Botswana, 3).

Once a state of emergency has been declared, the executive can suspend the people's exercise of their civil and political rights in the interest of state security. In a state of emergency it is common for the rules regarding preventive detention to be relaxed. In Zambia, the President can order the arrest and detention of any person when the President believes it necessary 'for the purpose of preserving public security' (Zambia, 39). In Egypt, a state of emergency not only authorises the executive branch to restrict most constitutional protection of individual liberties, but also authorises prosecution for violations of emergency regulations before state security courts, whose decisions are final and not subject to appeal or review by civil courts (Egypt, 9).

Derogation

Specific provisions of the constitution may be subject to derogation - that is, partial repeal or suspension - based on the operation of other constitutional provisions, during an emergency or for other reasons. For example, in Nigeria '[s]ection 41 of the 1979 Constitution provides circumstances under which the State could derogate from or restrict the rights to private and family life, freedom of thought, conscience and religion, expression and the press, peaceful assembly, association, and movement'–in short, most fundamental rights. Such derogation is supposed to occur by operation of a 'law that is reasonably justifiable in a democratic society for the interest of defence, public safety, public order, public morality, or public health, or for protecting the rights and freedom of other persons' (Nigeria, 23). However, restrictions on judicial review make it almost impossible to institute a legal challenge to verify whether a state of emergency is consistent with its declared rationale.

Ouster Provisions and Claw back Clauses

Ouster clauses preclude or 'oust' the jurisdiction of the courts over provisions of the constitution or other laws, thereby prohibiting them from hearing cases brought under the provisions in question. Ouster clauses can be found in the Nigerian constitution, prohibiting civil proceedings with respect to matters subject to governmental decrees or edicts (Nigeria, 26).

Claw back clauses permit constitutional provisions and guarantees to be restricted by ordinary legislation. They are common in Kenya (Kenya, 8-11), and in Zambia, where they supersede many civil liberties, as well as the operation of political parties and trade unions (Zambia, 41).

Customary and Religious Law

For the majority of Africans, customary law is the most important source of law and the type of law with which they are likely to have first and most frequent contact. Attitudes toward customary law and the relationship between customary law and the formal legal system vary widely among countries. Customary law is directly or indirectly recognised in almost all the legal systems studied in this project, but it plays varying roles in them. In a few countries, such as Botswana and South Africa (Botswana, 21-22; South Africa, 19), customary law is enshrined in the constitution. Botswana has established a customary court of appeal and a House of Chiefs. All legislation dealing with the 'designation, recognition, and removal' of chiefs and their subordinates; customary courts; customary law; and tribal property must be referred to the House of Chiefs (Botswana, 21-22). In many countries, customary law governs family law, property rights and other domestic matters (South Africa, 20; Uganda, 13) .

Governments often employ a variety of ways to circumscribe the role of customary law. Many countries studied subordinate customary law to their constitution and statutes. In Uganda, for example, customary law is not codified. It may be applied in official state courts, although it is subordinated there to statutory law and common law principles. When there is a conflict of laws, customary law must cede. In addition, according to Section 8(1) of the Judicature Act, customary law may not be 'repugnant to natural justice, equity and good conscience' (Uganda, 13-14). Botswana has established judicial mechanisms for the appeal of customary law decisions in statutory courts. In addition, in a number of countries, including South Africa, customary law has been made expressly subject to the non-discrimination provisions of the constitution (South Africa, 20).

It is possible for the legal system to recognise customary law, yet regulate it almost out of existence. In Kenya, for example, the Constitution recognises customary law in limited situations where the parties are from ethnic groups subject to it and there is no relevant statutory law. It cannot be invoked in criminal cases, and when it is applied it is subject to very strict conditions. To be applicable, customary law is subject to a 'repugnancy'[6]

---

6   In common law African countries the existence of customary law is always a matter to be proved. In addition to the evidentiary requirement of proof, the application of customary law was also made conditional on its passing a 'repugnancy test' requiring it not to be repugnant to natural justice, equity and good conscience nor contrary to a law (for the time being) in force or to public policy. With the adoption of constitutional bills of rights in most of these countries, the vague standards set by the repugnancy test/clause would now seem to have been supplanted by the clearer test of consistency with constitutionally entrenched rights.

test; it must be consistent with written law and of general local notoriety; and it must be devoid of internal conflicts (Kenya, 13).

Issues of religious law come to the fore in the intersection between Islamic law and the secular or civil legal system. In most countries with large or even majority Muslim populations, where *Shari'a* is part of the legal system, its ambit is limited to family law and the law of inheritance. This is not true in the Sudan, where the introduction of *Shari'a* by the government in 1983 has important human rights implications. The issues include whether *Shari'a*, as interpreted in Sudan, is compatible with human rights, in particular the rights of women; whether criticism of Sudan's human rights record is an attack on Islam and therefore punishable by death as apostasy or heresy; and whether Islamic law can be compatible with the secular legal values of 'multipartism, pluralism, minority rights, equality before the law and a citizenship-based doctrine of rights and obligations' (Sudan, 43). The Sudanese legal system has for a long time been divided into civil and *Shari'a* divisions, which traditionally have had a clear separation between their respective spheres. Since 1983, the lines of demarcation have become increasingly blurred, in favour of the expanded jurisdiction of religious judges. There has been a corresponding erosion of traditional common law principles, including professional responsibility and the rules of evidence and procedure (Sudan, 45).

Nigeria provides a different model for the relationship between religious and secular law. Although Nigeria has a large Muslim population, a series of military governments have regulated *Shari'a* the same way as non-religious customary law: it has imposed strict limits on it and subordinated it to the secular legal system. *Shari'a* law must be compatible with the Constitution; decisions from *Shari'a* courts can be appealed first to *Shari'a* courts of appeal and after that to the civil system; and *Shari'a* law is subject to supervision by the high courts in the secular system (Nigeria, 43).

In South Africa, where Muslims make up only one percent of the population, their treatment in the legal system is encompassed within the protections afforded to minorities. Although historically, Muslims in South Africa were not able to use their religious law to govern their personal relations, like many other aspects of South African law, this began to change in 1993. The 1996 Constitution recognises religious personal law, although this provision is too new to have been tested yet in court. Questions therefore still remain about the nature of its relationship to secular law and how it will ultimately be implemented, in particular with respect to the constitutional requirement not to discriminate against women (South Africa, 20-21).

The Judiciary and the Legal Profession

In this section, authors were requested to consider the institutional framework for the legal protection of human rights in their respective countries. They were first asked to explain and discuss the general structure and organisation of the judiciary, training of judges, and their institutional culture and professional traditions. They were also asked to assess the theory and reality of independence of the judiciary, past and present, as well as its prospects in the near term.

Authors were also asked to make a similar review of the structure and organisation of the legal profession and its role in the protection of human rights. Issues to address included an analysis of its composition, training, traditions, and organisations (e.g. bar associations); whether legal aid or legal services are provided for human rights cases or organisations; and whether the profession is involved in education or training for the legal protection of human rights.

Structure and Organisation of the Judiciary

As can be expected, there are significant differences between common and civil law jurisdictions with respect to the structure and organisation of the judiciary. In common law countries, the structures are fairly similar, although the terminology may vary. Usually there is a hierarchy of courts of generalised and specialised jurisdiction. The former hear both civil and criminal cases and are usually divided geographically, with district courts feeding into regional courts. Lower courts of general jurisdiction are often referred to as Magistrates' Courts. Limitations may be placed on lower courts in terms of the geographic area covered, subject matter jurisdiction, and size of the claim (Kenya, 14). Special jurisdiction courts, as their name implies, handle particular and well-defined areas of the law. In South Africa, for example, special jurisdiction courts hear certain criminal, labour and juvenile cases (South Africa, 21).

Common law systems derived from the British model usually have a

High Court, which has unlimited original jurisdiction over both civil and criminal cases and may also function as a constitutional court. The highest court in the system is usually the Court of Appeal, which will only rule on questions of law. There are exceptions, though. In Nigeria, Zambia and some other common law jurisdictions, there is a Supreme Court above the High Court (Zambia, 23).

Nigeria provides a good illustration of how this structure may be altered to deprive it of its inherent protections, in this case by the creation of military tribunals. These tribunals are major violators of human rights, and their decisions are subject neither to appeal nor judicial review (Nigeria, 41-42). They tend to overlook the rules of evidence, violate standard procedural protections and often rush to judgment (Nigeria, 41). The outcomes of cases with similar facts may vary greatly, depending on the 'political leanings of those involved' (Nigeria, 42). For example, Ken Saro-Wiwa and other activists were sentenced to death and hanged, while the death sentence of a retired general accused of similar offences and tried by the same tribunal was commuted to five years' imprisonment (Nigeria, 42).

In common law systems, judges' training is limited and frequently acquired on the job. Often, particularly in former British colonies such as Kenya, judges may be expatriates from other Commonwealth countries (Kenya, 15). In Uganda, a Judicial Training Committee is responsible for organising and implementing the training of judges. However, higher-level judges tend to receive only sporadic training. They may be reluctant to participate in training programmes if they perceive them as calling into question their competence. The magistrates, who make up the lower ranks of the judiciary, are more likely to receive ongoing and systematic training. However, the level of legal knowledge required for magistrates' positions is lower than that of higher level judges and it varies according to the magistrate's grade. Chief Magistrates and Grade I Magistrates must have professional legal qualifications, but only one year of specialised training in the law is required for Grade II and Grade III magistrates (Uganda, 15).

The judicial system of civil law countries bears some similarity to that of common law countries: the existence of a jurisdictional order and of specialised or emergency courts. The resemblance stops there, however, because, as soon as they acceded to international sovereignty, these countries substantially modified the judicial system (both European and indigenous) inherited from the French and Belgian colonisers. The changes, triggered to a large extent by budgetary problems and the extreme lack of qualified personnel which they faced, led eventually to the unification and simplification of the law in these newly independent States.

Indeed, in these countries, the courts of justice (civil and criminal) constitute a unified entity. Appellations vary from one country to another, but they are generally composed of Justices of the Peace, Courts of First Instance, Labour Courts, Criminal Courts, Courts of Appeal and Supreme Courts which, no matter what the status of the defendant is, judge all sorts of cases: civil, commercial, criminal or administrative.

Justices of the Peace[7] have a limited competence in civil matters, varying from country to country, and in criminal matters with regard to minor offences or certain criminal offences. Appeal from their decisions generally lies to Courts of First Instance[8] to which most of the competence of the customary or Muslim courts of the colonial period has been transferred. All these courts are composed of a single professional magistrate who examines and tries the cases. They also constitute, for the defendant, the first level of appeal and are thus referred to as First Degree or First Instance Tribunals.

The second degree of jurisdiction is composed of the Courts of Appeal. They are, in principle, intended to judge all the appeals against judgments passed in the first resort by first degree tribunals, but also hear some of the administrative lawsuits, as a result of the suppression of the administrative courts. They operate in a collegial form (in general, a President and two assistants both of whom are professional magistrates) and are divided into civil, commercial and criminal chambers. There are also specialised or emergency courts which operate according to the same rules as Criminal Courts (for trying criminals), such as State Security Courts (for all cases involving the breach of national security), and Courts of Budget Discipline (to try cases relative to the execution of the State Budget).

At the top of the hierarchy, we find the Supreme Courts. Inspired by the model of the 1957 Supreme Court of Morocco, they have jurisdictional attributions (control of the constitutionality of laws, appeal against decisions emanating from administrative authorities and appeal to the Court of Cassation against judgments passed in the last resort) to which some constitutions have added consultative functions. They were originally divided into sections (constitutional, administrative, judicial and financial). But many countries later transformed the constitutional section into a Constitutional Court while others simply duplicated the French model

---

7 Departmental Courts in Senegal and in Mauritania, Canton Courts in Rwanda or Residence Court in Burundi.

8 Regional Courts in Senegal and in Mauritania, Higher Instance Courts in Mali.

which comprises a Constitutional Court, a Court of Cassation (for criminal and civil cases), a State Court (for administrative appeals) and a National Audit Court (for financial cases). Moreover, almost all these countries have a High Court of Justice composed, very often, of professional magistrates and elected representatives (members of Parliament), responsible for trying high authorities of the State for misdemeanours committed in the exercise of their functions.

The law applicable in these countries has not changed much even though efforts have been made to formulate and adopt new codes and laws in the field of criminal and civil law. Besides, in most constitutions, it is stated that the laws and regulations in force at the time of their promulgation 'will remain in force until they are modified or repealed'.

The separation of powers and the independence of the judiciary are also provided for in all French-speaking constitutions. But the issue here is that the judiciary is considered as 'a simple State service like are health and education, with, in addition, special guarantees for the magistrates who pass judgment, and only in the exercise of their functions.'[9] Thus the use of the expression 'judicial authority' in place of 'judiciary', which is constitutionally very loaded, but also the institution of constitutional protection for judges who are subject only to the authority of the law. This independence is recognised, for some judges, by the principle of irremovability, meaning that a judge cannot be transferred, even on promotion, without his consent.

In civil law countries, there are two categories of magistrates (or judges). *Magistrats assis* (sitting judges) are responsible for giving judgments in litigation while *magistrats debouts* (standing judges, or magistrates of the prosecution) represent the interests of society. In this capacity, they are responsible for criminal proceedings and direct the activities of the gendarmes and police when the latter exercise the functions of judicial police officers.

The magistrates have a special status: they are recruited on the basis of their qualifications (generally lawyers with a given number of years of experience, university professors and certain officials in the Justice administration with legal diplomas and a few years experience) and/or by competitive examination. They pursue training in a specialised institution[10] for a period that varies from one country to another but, generally, does not exceed two years. This training leads to the award of a national diploma.

9 See Keba-Mbaye, 'Contentieux judiciaire' in *L'organisation judiciaire, la procedure civile et les voies d'execution*, Vol IV, *Encyclopedie de l'Afrique*, 41.

10 During the first years after independence, the training was pursued in France but since the mid-1980s, several countries (including Senegal, Ivory Coast, Burkina Faso) have created training institutes for magistrates which are often of a sub-regional character.

They also receive continuing education which can take place partly in France or in Belgium. The magistrates' profession (code of practice, promotion, disciplinary measures, etc.) is administered by an institution known as the High Council of the Magistracy which is, in general, presided over by the President of the Republic. In the exercise of their profession, they are bound by the duty of confidentiality, i.e. they cannot have a hostile attitude towards the authorities of their country and should observe the greatest neutrality between the parties in a trial. In some countries, such as Senegal, legislation even forbids them to be members of a political party or a trade union.

Judicial Independence

An independent judiciary is indispensable for the legal protection of human rights. Here again, the reports present a mixed picture. While judicial independence exists and is protected on paper, in practice it can be undermined in two principal ways. The first is the actual dependence of judges on the executive branch of the government for their job security. The second refers to restrictions on judicial power to decide cases. Most of the countries studied have established the structural independence of the judiciary in the form of separation of powers. However, exceptions exist. Prior to adoption of the 1990 Constitution, formal separation of powers did not exist in Mozambique, and the judiciary was subject to the influence of the Ministry of Justice (Mozambique, 16-17).

Despite the formal separation of powers, the judiciary is subject to executive power. Judges are almost invariably appointed by the executive branch of government, and therefore depend on the executive branch for their jobs, even in cases where nominally independent bodies such as Judicial Service Commissions make the actual nominations. Lower-level judges may be appointed by designated agencies within the executive branch. In general, the highest level judges - those on the High Court and above - are nominated by the chief executive. In some countries the nomination is subject to legislative confirmation, while in others it is not.

Security of tenure exists on paper, but is easily circumvented in practice. In theory, judges may only be removed for cause, and removal procedures exist in most of the jurisdictions studied. Nevertheless, there is considerable scope for discretion and interpretation in invoking and utilising these procedures, which has the effect of depriving them of their force. In a few countries, executive control of judicial tenure is complete, open and explicitly provided by the legal system. The best example among the countries studied is Sudan, where judges serve at the pleasure of the President of the Republic, who has complete power to appoint, discipline and remove them, simply by invoking the public interest (Sudan, 45-46). In most countries, the control is less visible, and is effected through manipulation of administrative processes, often on a case-by-case basis. In Kenya, for example, the executive branch has at its disposal a variety of ways to punish judges who have displeased it, including transfers to undesirable locations and failure to renew their contracts (Kenya, 15-18). Similarly, in Morocco, the executive can suspend a magistrate accused of serious error or transfer a magistrate to 'any vacant post in the kingdom at any time.' In theory, a judge can be transferred without consent for a maximum period of three months; in practice, it is difficult for magistrates to withhold their consent. (Morocco, 20-21).

Judicial dependence on the executive branch is also fostered by the inadequacy of their salaries and pensions. This has the effect of making judges less willing to alienate the executive branch, for fear of poverty after retirement. Retired judges often continue to serve as judges on contract. Employment by means of a renewable contract is clearly incompatible with judicial independence (Zambia, 15). The need for judges to curry favour with the executive power, whatever the original motivation, will sooner or later fatally compromise the quality of judicial performance.

Judges may also be incompetent or corrupt. Corruption is a common way of dealing with low salaries. Nigeria provides a clear illustration of these difficulties. Material and equipment, such as stationery and typewriters (much less computers!) are lacking, and judges take note of the proceedings in longhand. Their salaries are low and payment is often delayed. A typical judge on a state high court earns the equivalent of US $1,000 per year, and salaries are correspondingly smaller for lower court judges and administrative personnel at all levels. As a result of the severe financial constraints and the low level of professionalism generally, court personnel, including magistrates, extort money from litigants. A panel investigating judicial practices submitted recommendations for reform in 1995, but the government has yet to take action (Nigeria, 46). In Uganda there is a widespread public perception that the judicial system is corrupt and that favourable judgments can be purchased (Uganda, 25).

The second type of limitation on judicial power occurs when the pressure is applied to judges' authority, rather than to their job security, in the form of overt or subtle pressure to decide a case in a particular way. Judges' ability to apply the law effectively or well is also circumscribed by a lack of resources across the board: dockets are crowded, courtroom facilities are inadequate, delays are frequent, and there is a general lack of access to case reporters and other sources of legal precedent, which are necessary for adequate judicial performance in common law jurisdictions. Dissemination of decisions that could be useful in human rights cases is random or inadequate.

Countries with common law legal systems willingly draw on precedents from other common law jurisdictions, and not just in Africa, provided they know about them. International law is also invoked, although less often. An example is the 1992 *Unity Dow* case from Botswana, in which the Court of Appeal struck down the section of the Botswana citizenship act preventing women from transmitting their citizenship to their children, by holding that the citizenship law contravened CEDAW, which Botswana had ratified (Botswana, 10; Nigeria, 29).

Rwanda offers an extreme example of the challenges facing a historically weak and dependent judicial system, struggling to cope with the staggering caseload of prosecutions resulting from the 1994 genocide. Like every part of Rwandan society, the judicial system itself was a victim of the genocide; much of its infrastructure and many of its records were destroyed, and its own personnel were not exempt from the killing. Since the genocide of April-July 1994, prisons are now seriously overcrowded and judicial procedures, especially relating to arrest and detention, have tended to be 'irregular.' To deal with the backlog of cases there has been a tendency to 'trivialise' crimes not related to genocide or massacres, that is, to reduce the offence charged to eliminate the need for prosecution or imprisonment upon conviction. Most of the prosecutors' offices and cantonal courts did not begin to operate until 1996. In spite of this, the judicial system has been functioning since then. New judicial institutions have been established, including reinstatement of the Supreme Court and the creation of a Supreme Council of Judges, that are expected to reduce the executive branch's traditional ability to control the judicial system (Rwanda, 18-20).

The Legal Profession
Most lawyers are trained at in-country law schools, which offer a standard

curriculum. Law schools in a few countries offer courses in human rights; Uganda is one of them (Uganda, 18). Access to the legal profession may be restricted in some countries that require lawyers to serve a training period as articled clerks before they can practice on their own and the number of placements is limited. This is a problem in South Africa, where the number of placements is sufficient to meet only 60 percent of the demand. In response, legislation has been passed, allowing candidates to train in other settings, such as community law clinics. So far, this has happened only on a small scale (South Africa, 55). Kenya has responded to the same constraint by scrapping the requirement for articles of clerkship, replacing it with a combination of a year's apprenticeship under a senior advocate and additional formal education, followed by an examination (Kenya, 19).

Not surprisingly, the independence of local bar associations, along with their willingness to take human rights cases and provide assistance to human rights organisations, is consistent with the general climate for human rights in the country. In relatively open countries, bar associations and lawyers generally have more scope to litigate on behalf of human rights. In Uganda, all lawyers must belong to the Uganda Law Society, a statutorily created body, which sponsors a Legal Aid Project focusing on the promotion and protection of human rights. However, the Uganda report criticises the legal community for remaining 'largely silent on major or sensitive human rights issues,' noting that the battle for human rights in Uganda has been waged through education and not the legal system. Another reason for the relative passivity of the Ugandan bar is that lawyers in Uganda, as in other parts of the world, tend to be middle class and conservative and are therefore less likely to challenge the status quo. This is not true, however, of women lawyers in Uganda, who have helped to lead the struggle for women's human rights through the 'very active and dynamic' Ugandan Association of Women Lawyers (Uganda, 19).

In repressive countries, where lawyers, like other potential challengers of the system, are themselves at considerable risk, they are less likely to take cases that could get them in trouble or threaten their livelihood. For example, lawyers in Nigeria have a realistic fear of being stigmatised if they take human rights cases (Nigeria, 48). In the Sudan, the Bar Association, established in 1935, distinguished itself in its advocacy of civil and political rights; members of the Bar Association often volunteered to represent individuals accused of political crimes. This earned it the hostility of the government, which shut it down in 1989, along with trade and other associations (Sudan, 47).

Access to the legal system, particularly for poor, rural and other disenfranchised people, is also a problem. Lawyers are expensive and their fees are beyond the reach of most potential litigants. The legal system is usually elitist, or perceived as such, and its practitioners are concentrated in the cities, beyond the reach of the largely poor rural population. Public defenders, if found at all, are available only to criminal defendants in serious cases. At present, poor litigants in civil cases must rely on *pro bono* lawyers and legal aid societies, if available. Legal aid societies do exist in some countries - Uganda is one example - but their resources are inadequate to meet the demand.

In South Africa, the impetus to meet the need for legal services originates with the government. The Ministry of Justice, in response to legislation, has created a government-funded Legal Aid Board, whose goal is 'to render or make available legal aid to indigent persons' (South Africa, 35-36). However, as with many other aspects of the 'new South Africa,' the government's goals far exceed its capacity to fund them. Partly in response to criticism of the Legal Aid Board's inability to meet the demand for its services, a pilot project is now underway to assess the feasibility of starting a public defender system. South Africa is also exhibiting considerable creativity by experimenting with other, less expensive ways of delivering legal services to those who need them. The Legal Aid Board has established several Community Centres, housed at universities, to provide legal assistance in both civil and criminal matters. In addition, the Board is discussing joint initiatives with non-governmental organisations (NGOs) (South Africa, 37). As another way to increase people's access to legal services, the South African legal system relies on the use of para-legals (South Africa, 40-41, 56-57).

Mozambique presents an interesting case, because of the major transitions that its legal system, like South Africa's, has undergone since the early 1990s. At independence, only five of about 350 Portuguese legal practitioners remained in the country. In response, the government banned private law practice and allowed law students and paralegals to practice law. However, since 1994, with the establishment of the Mozambican Bar Association and the legalisation of private law practice, the legal profession has become more like that in other African countries. Under this new system, access to adequate legal assistance is still a problem. The vast majority of the

200 lawyers in Mozambique are concentrated in the capital, Maputo, and the role of legal counsel in district courts is left to *ad hoc* 'public defenders,' who have no legal background at all (Mozambique, 20-22).

The Political, Social and Economic Context

After presenting the normative and institutional frameworks for the legal protection of human rights in the two preceding sections, authors were requested to situate the current practice and future prospects in a general political, cultural and economic context. This is important in order to understand better how these formal normative and institutional frameworks function in actual practice and operation. In this section authors were also asked to consider the current role and operation of customary law, where applicable, especially as a possible source of human rights violations, and assess its future prospects in view of wider political, social and economic developments.

An important political factor is the presence of unrest or insurrection and the impact on human rights that such unrest can have in the affected area and throughout the country. Such a situation can provide the government with an excuse to declare a state of emergency or otherwise constrict civil and political rights. It can also legitimise a military or authoritarian government in the name of national security or preservation of the territorial integrity of the country.

Obvious economic factors include gross disparities between rich and poor. The overwhelming majority of the population is grindingly poor, and governments are all too often an institutionalised form of thievery of the country's wealth. In addition, externally imposed requirements, notably structural adjustment programmes, can have a significant negative impact on social, economic and cultural rights (Morocco, 17-18).

Some widespread social problems can have negative consequences for the legal protection of human rights. For example, the Kenya and South Africa studies highlight the importance of literacy training in any effort to promote human rights (Kenya, 26; South Africa, 58). Given the reality of massive illiteracy, the challenge is to devise effective non-literate ways of promoting a culture of engaged and assertive awareness of human rights standards among the illiterate majority, and to motivate the literate elite to take the protection of human rights seriously.

One of the major human rights problems mentioned in practically all of the studies is discrimination against women, which was most often discussed in terms of customary and religious law. The Uganda study highlights the gender bias and discrimination that women encounter in formal legal systems as well. The second-class status of women in the broader society - their higher levels of poverty and lack of access to land, for example - find their echo in the judicial system and make it harder for them to expect fair treatment from it (Uganda, 25-26). A number of discriminatory laws are still on the books, even though they violate the anti-discrimination provisions of the Constitution (Uganda, 26). Partly as a result of their dissatisfaction with the formal system, women have tended to use the Local Council courts, which are set up to resolve minor disputes at the village, parish and sub-county level (Uganda, 15), and are therefore more accessible and less expensive than the formal system. However, women are subject to discrimination at the Local Council level also. These courts usually apply customary law, which is often biased against women. In addition, judges in the Local Council courts are almost all men from the local community, who share the biases of their milieu; have little or no training; lack knowledge of the law; and therefore, often make 'partial and uninformed decisions' (Uganda, 25-26).

With respect to the application of customary law, the question is not whether it is possible or desirable to replace it by statutory or state law in the abstract. Rather, it is the relationship between the application of customary law and the legal protection of human rights that is at issue. At one level, since customary law will probably be perceived by local populations as more culturally authentic, accessible, and useful than the externally imposed colonial legal systems, its forcible displacement may itself constitute a human rights violation. Statutory legal systems are incapable of properly serving urban populations, let alone the rural populations who have even less access to them and are less able to afford their costs. Neither are they conceived or implemented in ways that are necessarily more protective of human rights than customary law. But the cultural authenticity or practical expediency of customary law should never be upheld at the expense of effective protection of human rights, especially the human rights of women, who suffer most under various customary and religious law systems. The challenge is therefore how to regulate the content and application of customary and religious law in order to better protect and promote human rights in local communities.

The 'new' South Africa provides a good illustration of the kinds of difficulties a benevolent - even progressive - government can face in trying to ensure the legal protection of human rights. The situation in South Africa is different from the other African countries studied in at least two respects. First, the government is actively supporting the population, and human rights are enshrined and institutionalised throughout the new system. Because the government is a help, not a hindrance, there is much scope for creativity and innovative approaches. In terms of the problems being recognised and addressed, South Africa appears to be well ahead of the other countries. Second, the principal human rights problem South Africa is facing right now is the persistence of the past into the present. The country is attempting to deal with its ugly legacy, and that is raising a host of difficult questions, many of which are considered in the country study: the question of amnesty and forgiveness of the past; the work of the Truth and Reconciliation Commission and other commissions; the gross disparities between rich and poor, white and black, urban and rural; the contradictions inherent in being simultaneously a rich, industrialised country and a poor developing country; and the continuing economic, social, cultural and other deformities caused by generations of a hateful racial caste system.

The situation is less optimistic in Rwanda, another country struggling with the present and future implications of a violent and divided past. Even though the extreme historical circumstances of South Africa or Rwanda are not reproduced in the other countries submitting reports, these countries may also someday face the difficult and delicate issue of forgiveness for former oppressors still living in their midst. South Africa's willingness at least to grapple with the question may provide an instructive example for the whole continent, while the recent history of Rwanda graphically illustrates the potential consequences of failing to do so.

Status and Role of Non-Governmental Organisations

Having discussed the theory and practice of the *formal legal system*, authors were then invited to discuss and evaluate the *informal sector*, namely the status and role of NGOs, whether they identify themselves as 'human rights' organisations or not. Issues to be considered here included the mandate, constituency (popular support), operational capacity, funding, and accountability of local or national NGOs, as well as their networks and future prospects. Authors were asked to consider whether NGOs could survive and be effective without external funding and technical assistance, and to analyse the relationship between local or national NGOs, on the one hand, and international NGOs and foreign governments, especially of Europe and North America, on the other.

The authors' reactions to NGOs were mixed. NGOs were criticised as elitist, alienated from the population, or ineffective. According to the Kenya study, NGO activities centre around a 'professional seminar circuit' in the urban areas (Kenya, 21-22). Another common criticism is that, as a result of external factors, such as restrictions imposed by governments (Botswana, 22; Kenya, 21-22), or internal realities, such as the lack of resources, NGOs have little impact on the problems they seek to address. NGOs are also subject to criticism for lack of co-ordination amongst themselves and consequent duplication of effort. In response, in some countries such as Uganda, where the climate is favourable, NGOs have begun to work together: to network; co-ordinate their activities; share information, training and other resources; and lobby the government and international donors (Uganda, 29-30).

The non-governmental human rights structure often reflects the circumstances and political divisions in the country. In Morocco, for example, there are three national human rights NGOs: the oldest one is associated with Islam and religious law, a second was founded by 'various left-wing militant groups,' and the most recent is a secular organisation established under the aegis of the Bar Association (Morocco, 25-26). In 1990, all three organisations began working together and, along with the Bar Association, developed a national charter for human rights, which was signed in 1990. The three groups have continued to work together, although all have had difficulty institutionalising their efforts in the face of numerous challenges to the human rights situation in Morocco, including government hostility, widespread destitution and resistance to change. Internally, organisational effectiveness is reduced by lack of training, managerial and administrative capacity, and funding. Because their initial efforts are often met with failure, the NGOs employ a variety of methods, both inside and outside the legal system, to exert pressure. These include issuing communiqués and reports, observing court cases, monitoring compliance with international human rights conventions, and working with and through the media and international NGOs (Morocco, 27).

Most of the studies that criticised NGOs also acknowledged a positive role for them. The role of NGOs may be more highly valued in countries that are, to a greater or lesser degree, inimical to human rights. The Nigeria study, for example, criticised NGOs for being urban and elitist, but noted that this orientation has begun to change since 1993, as a result of the work of the community-based environmental movement in the oil-producing region of the country. The Nigeria report praises the courage of human rights and pro-democracy NGOs, many of whose members were detained or killed in the successful effort to drive President Babangida from office and the (so far) less successful effort to restore democratic government (Nigeria, 52-53).

In Rwanda, most NGOs are very new, having originated after 1990, and they lack institutional experience and history. However, many of them have experienced staff members, who have solid and positive accomplishments to their credit, achieved under very difficult circumstances. Staff members of some Rwandan NGOs were targeted by the Habyarimana regime during the massacres and were among its first victims. Relations with the current government are much improved. Some Rwandan NGOs have denounced human rights abuses, provided accurate reports on the human rights situation in the country, and conducted human rights training and sensitisation. Traditionally, Rwandan NGOs have not been oriented toward the legal system, but this may be changing; some NGOs have announced plans to provide legal assistance to victims of the genocide and even to those accused of perpetrating it (Rwanda, 30-31).

Uganda exemplifies the kinds of difficulties NGOs can face even in a country with a relatively good human rights record. In the last ten years, with the improved climate for human rights and the strengthening of civil society in Uganda, the number of NGOs and community-based organisations has grown very rapidly. NGOs are required to register with the NGO Board, a governmental entity. Many NGOs find the registration requirements burdensome and view them as a way for the government to monitor and possibly control the activities of NGOs it does not like. Many organisations active in promoting civil, political, economic, social and cultural human rights identify themselves as development rather than human rights organisations. This is due in part to the fact that groups working in the economic and social area often do not view their work through a human rights framework. Other NGOs, working in traditional areas of human rights concern, have tried to avoid the human rights label because of the risk of having their activities viewed as 'political' or 'subversive' by the government (Uganda, 29). In spite of these negatives, the Uganda report views the future prospects for NGOs as good, provided they become more responsive and accountable to local communities. This will not happen until NGOs become less dependent on foreign donors and more reliant on local sources of funding and support (Uganda, 29-30).

Most of the studies did not discuss the relationship between local NGOs and either international NGOs or their donors in the North. The Senegal study identified most of the human rights organisations in the country as local branches of international NGOs or United Nations agencies (Senegal, 14-15). There is broad agreement among the authors of the country studies who did address the question that NGOs are dependent on foreign sources of funding, training and technical assistance at the present time, and are likely to remain so for the foreseeable future. Several studies suggested that NGOs are likely to tailor their programmes to conform to donors' funding preferences (Kenya, 21; Uganda, 29). The situation is similar in Rwanda but has a slightly different spin. Cooperation between Rwandan and northern NGOs tends to be limited to funding and training. According to the Rwanda country study, northern organisations have been wary of Rwandan NGOs, suspecting them, most often incorrectly, of partisanship and lack of impartiality (Rwanda, 31).

Concluding Remarks

Since, as noted earlier, the preceding synthesis does not cover even all those countries identified for study by the Lusaka Planning Meeting, there is no basis at this stage of the project for final or general conclusions about the status of the legal protection of human rights in Africa at large. But this is neither surprising nor problematic for this project. As suggested in Chapter 1 above, this continental initiative should seek to mediate between two poles: the multi-faceted diversity of Africa on the one hand, and the similarity of the experiences of its peoples with colonialism and its aftermath on the other. Due regard to the cultural, ethnic, religious, and other diversities of African societies counsels against generalisation. Yet the similarities of recent African experiences are too obvious and relevant to ignore in efforts to combine resources and develop responses to the far-reaching consequences of past colonialism and current globalisation. In this light, one should expect to find, and can indeed find in my view, some clear patterns, themes and similarities in the preceding review of some country studies, rather than hard and fast general conclusions.

Even if or to the extent that some general conclusions can be draw from the studies reviewed above, I suggest that is not the primary objective of this project as a whole. In my view, the object is not to analyse and characterise the status of the legal protection of human rights for academic or scholarly purposes. Rather, it is to understand the possibilities and limitations of this approach in the present context of each in order to devise and implement better strategies for the protection and promotion of human rights in all African countries. As explained in the Report of the Lusaka Planning Meeting, methods of legal protection should neither be considered in isolation from the social, economic and political context of African societies in which they are supposed to apply, nor be assumed to be sufficient by themselves for the effective implementation of human rights standards. By focusing on legal protection, this project seeks to take a realistic yet visionary view of the practical possibilities and limitations of these mechanisms and institutions *only as part of* a broad range of strategies for the implementation of human rights in African societies.

Chapter 4

An Assessment of
Information and Training Resources

Chidi Anselm Odinkalu and Ibrahima Kane[1]

This report provides a mapping of the technical resource and support bases in the areas of information and training at the disposal of or accessible to groups, institutions and individuals working to protect human rights through law in Africa. It was initially prepared as part of a project on the legal protection of human rights under the constitutions of Africa, which was initiated following requests by advocates, activists and judges in Africa, and undertaken in consultation with them. The report presents a summary description of the types and categories of information and training resources available to support the legal protection of human rights, attempts an assessment of their utility and identifies areas of need. It also proposes recommendations for greater intra-African co-operation in the areas of training and information resource support and exchange.

Background

The mandate for this report is derived from the deliberations of the Lusaka planning meeting for the project.[2] The planning meeting operationalised the meaning of 'legal protection' to include 'all activities that are incidental to legal protection of human rights such as information dissemination, capacity building and legislative advocacy.'[3] Amongst those activities it emphasised, in particular, information exchange and training. The planning meeting identified 'the poor capacity of civil society and public institutions' as one of the major obstacles to the protection of human rights through law in Africa. It referred specifically to the following elements:

---

1   The authors acknowledge the invaluable assistance of Clinton Light of the Legal Assistance Centre (LAC), Namibia; Desmond Kaunda, of the Danish Centre for Human Rights, Malawi; Lucrecia Seafield of the European Human Rights Foundation, South Africa; Hisham Mubarak, formerly of the Centre for Human Rights Legal Aid, Egypt; Romana Cacchioli and Emma Playfair of INTERIGHTS, United Kingdom. Hisham Mubarak passed away in January 1998, shortly after the completion of the first draft of this report.

2   See Introduction, above, and *The Legal Protection of Human Rights Under the Constitutions of Africa: Report of Planning Meeting, Lusaka, Zambia, 28 - 30 July, 1995,* prepared by Chidi Anselm Odinkalu, and available at INTERIGHTS' offices in London.

3   Ibid. at 11.

(a) lack of professionalism and the presence of poorly equipped, poorly trained and, in some cases, unqualified legal and judicial personnel wielding enormous powers and discretion over the life, limb, property and reputation of others. In most countries, there is no continuing legal/judicial education…;

(b) the absence of [a capacity for] proper planning in public institutions, resulting in absence of defined goals, procedures and public confidence;

(c) the absence of law reports, indigenous legal texts, published compilations of applicable statutes, treaties and records of customary law;

(d) reliance on antiquated legal texts and rules which make the judicial process both complicated and abstruse; and

(e) inaccessibility of judicial records as a result of reliance on cumbersome judicial recording methods.[4]

To address these obstacles, the planning meeting, in addition to commissioning the country studies synthesized in Chapter 3 above, created two working groups, the first 'to assess and evaluate relevant training needs and facilities existing in Africa', and the second 'to assess existing information exchange among African NGOs and formulate proposals for gathering, organising and disseminating legal developments about human rights in Africa on a sustainable basis.' Both working groups, which subsequently merged into one working group, were authorised to undertake the 'widest possible consultation'[5] on these identified thematic areas in order to inform their report.[6]

Sources

This report has been prepared on the basis of information gathered by the Working Group and provided by sources that responded to requests for information on national practice in the different African countries. Recognising the vast diversity of Africa and the immense difficulties of communication within and across its various national boundaries, this report

---

4 Ibid. at 16.

5 Ibid. at 19.

6 The working groups were initially established as separate task groups. Ngande Mwanajiti, Executive Director of AFRONET, and Joanna Stevens, then Legal Information Officer at INTERIGHTS, constituted the information working group. The members of the working group on training were Bibiane Mbaye, Programme Officer at the Union for African Population Studies in Dakar, Senegal; Amir Salem, Executive Director of the Cairo-based Legal Research and Resources Centre for Human Rights; and Chidi Anselm Odinkalu, Legal Officer for Africa at INTERIGHTS. The working groups later merged into one project working group on information and training. They also co-opted three new members: Nana K. A. Busia, Jr., then West Africa researcher at the International Secretariat of Amnesty International in London; Ibrahima Kane, then Director of Information at the Dakar-based Rencontre Africaine pour la Défense des Droits de l'Homme; and Hisham

does not claim to be comprehensive. Rational expediency guided the choice of material and information. While every effort was made in its preparation to consult as widely as possible, we have been able to include in this chapter only those trends and developments known to or discovered by Working Group members in the limited time available to us, or brought to our attention by those colleagues who responded to our request for help, information and guidance. It is therefore illustrative rather than comprehensive, but we hope it succeeds in identifying key resources, deficiencies and needs.

The preparation of this report has benefited from diverse sources. First, several individuals and organisations agreed to evaluate and provide information on the relevant resources in their own jurisdictions, based on a checklist prepared and issued by the Working Group. We received such reports from Egypt, Ghana, Kenya, Malawi, Morocco, Namibia, Senegal, South Africa, Togo, and more generally for 'francophone'[7] West Africa. The task of the Working Group also entailed an evaluation of law reports and law reporting in the common law jurisdictions of Africa.[8] In addition, some of the country reports synthesised by Abdullahi An-Na'im above provided valuable information for this report.[9] We drew also on published secondary material, and on-line research into African legal information sources on the Internet. Finally, in some cases, interviews and correspondence with experts and practitioners in target jurisdictions supplemented available information.

The Context for This Report

The context for this report is defined by three principal factors:

> *The diversity of dominant legal traditions in Africa*, which, after colonialism, have mostly developed as mutations of the metropolitan legal systems.[10] The better known of these traditions are the civil law traditions of those countries which gained their independence from France and the common law traditions of those countries which gained their independence from the United Kingdom. These systems continue to be impacted in far reaching - if varying - degrees by traditional practices and rules of customary law.

Mubarak, then Executive Director of the Centre for Human Rights Legal Aid in Cairo. This larger working group met once in January 1997. Ngande Mwanajiti participated in this meeting, but was otherwise unable to contribute to this report. Joanna Stevens left the Working Group on leaving INTERIGHTS in July 1996.

7   'francophone' is used here as a term of convenience only.

8   The evaluation of law reporting was limited to common law jurisdictions because civil law jurisdictions do not habitually rely on law reports, as judicial decisions do not generally have value as precedent. This was nevertheless extended to cover those civil law jurisdictions which have some form of law reporting.

9   For a list of these countries, see Chapter 3, n. 4, *supra*.

10   This is also largely true of countries like Egypt, Liberia, and South Africa where the legal systems have been greatly shaped by Napoleonic, American and Roman-Dutch/Common Law influences respectively.

The geopolitics of Africa as a result of which the concept of statehood and the state in Africa remain both contested and contentious. The co-existence within the boundaries of the states of Africa of multiple ethnic and national identities creates a problem of constitutional power sharing which is yet to be satisfactorily resolved in an overwhelming majority of these states. This has produced several results relevant to this report. First, it has resulted in repressive and unaccountable governments around Africa three of whose consequences are worth mentioning here. First, the existence of repressive governments results in massive and systematic violations of human rights to such an extent that the legal machinery is ill-equipped to deal with them. Second, more often than not, repression begins with the evisceration of the legal process or the implementation by the executive branch of measures designed to undermine the ability of the judiciary to function credibly. Third, in a significant number of African states, systematic repression has resulted in civil conflict that, in turn, breeds further violations of human rights. In such situations, primacy is almost always accorded to finding political solutions, in preference to legal or judicial approaches, to redressing individual violations.

Related to the multiplicity of ethnic and national identities and arising from them, traditional practice and customary law remains a feature of all legal systems in Africa and raises unique dilemmas for the protection of human rights in the continent.[11] Existing theoretically under the Constitution, customary law often operates or owes its legitimacy outside it because of the political consequences that follow any attempts to transform or change it too quickly. These norms of tradition and customary law are invariably a substantial part of larger fabrics of micro-national identities in reference to which members of ethnic and national groups define themselves in the multi-national states that make up Africa. As a source of law, one difficulty with verifying or applying ethnic customary law, quite apart from the fact that it varies from place to place, is that it is mostly unwritten. In addition to ethnic customary law, norms of Islamic *Shari'a* exist and are administered in one way or another in over half of the states of Africa.

Ethiopia is the oldest of the states in Africa and the one in which these metropolitan influences are most minimal. Following independence in or around 1975, the former colonies of Portugal in Africa attempted to evolve their own indigenous legal systems by synthesising disparate legal traditions. That this process remains an ongoing experiment is evidenced by Mozambique's recent entry into the Commonwealth.

11 For an early and authoritative description of the reach of customary law in Africa, see, T.O. Elias, *The Nature of Customary Law in Africa* (Manchester University Press, 1956).

12 38 (39 if one includes the Saharawi Arab Democratic Republic) of the 54 countries in Africa have per capita GNP of less than $765 per annum. See *Human Development Report*, (United Nations Development Programme (UNDP), 1998), 225.

The economic and social reality in Africa, which provides the context for the legal protection of human rights. Harsh living conditions have been reinforced over the past decade by the adverse consequences of economic structural adjustment programmes implemented by most African governments - most of them genuinely unaccountable to their people - under the supervision of international financial institutions.[12] These conditions have been further worsened by the adverse consequences of mal-administration and corruption perpetrated by unaccountable governments and by an unsustainable debt overhang, itself a consequence of corruption. The consequences of this situation are felt at two different levels. At the individual level, increasing poverty becomes ever more pervasive and puts the legal and judicial process out of the reach of all but the most affluent members of the community. In response to such conditions, self-help is often the preferred strategy for protecting rights. At the governmental level, budgetary appropriations for the judiciary and the legal process are grossly inadequate to support even minimum efficiency, resulting in poor conditions of tenure and service and low morale among judicial personnel. While the vision of this project, and of this report in particular, is forward-looking, this present reality should be kept in mind, if only to underscore the challenges that this project will face well into the future.

For too long, judges, advocates, activists and other interested persons and institutions working to advance the protection of human rights through law in Africa have been limited to the resources available within their respective national jurisdictions, only occasionally making fleeting acquaintance with one another at forums usually organised by better resourced organisations in the North. This situation has been created, reinforced and sustained by a combination of factors.

First, historical divisions arising out of the colonial experiences of the different countries of Africa have persisted well into the present day. The legal systems and cultures of the various countries of Africa have largely developed as mutations of the metropolitan legal systems.[13] The former colonial powers themselves still commit considerable effort and resources to

---

13 This is also largely the case in Egypt, Liberia and South Africa, which were theoretically spared the colonial experience as such. It is much less true of Ethiopia. The Egyptian legal system, in particular, is the product of diverse influences, including British, French, Ottoman and Islamic legal traditions. For an account of the influences that shaped the development of the legal system of Egypt see, B. A. Robertson, 'The Emergence of the Modern Judiciary in the Middle East: Negotiating the Mixed Courts of Egypt,' in Chibli Mallat, ed., *Islam and Public Law: Classical and Contemporary Studies* (London: Graham & Trotman, 1992), 107-39.

14 For instance, a project - *Projet d'Appui à la Réforme du Système Judiciaire* (PARSJ) (Project to Support Reform of the Judicial System) - financed by France since 1996, provides funding for reinforcing French legal and judicial culture in the training of judges in francophone Africa. The OHADA (Organisation de l'Harmonisation du Droit des Affaires) (Organisation for the Harmonisation of Commercial Law) Treaty of 17 October 1993 brings together the countries of Africa which have French as their official language (including Mauritius) to harmonise their private law, ostensibly in order to give security to commercial

sustaining these differences, thereby reinforcing their own dominance in the legal systems and cultures of African countries and hindering efforts at horizontal exchange and integration within Africa.[14]

The differences in legal traditions, especially between the common law and civil law systems, are often cited to explain perceived disparities in attitudes toward the domestic application of international human rights norms. As Professor Abdelkader Boye of Cheikh Anta Diop University in Dakar, Senegal, explains:

> [T]he attitude of the municipal judge towards customary norms and even towards the principles of international public law is [not] easy to determine, a fact that is largely due to the unwritten nature of such norms. Yet another factor is the legal background (common law or Romano-Germanic law) of the judge, which plays a far from negligible role in his consideration of the customary rules of international public law. A reading of certain decisions of American or English courts suggests that they are more inclined than French courts, for example, to refer to customary norms or the general principles of international public law. One thing is certain, however: in no state do courts flatly decline to apply certain customary rules of international law. The fundamental differences as between one country and another reside in the manner in which those rules are understood and must be applied.'[15]

Politically, both the Cold War and the strict adherence by the member states of the Organisation of African Unity (OAU) to the principle of non-interference in the domestic affairs of other states ensured that accountability and remedies for violations of human rights did not rank high in the priorities of African states. The processes of domestic lawmaking and enforcement (as expressions of the sovereignty of states) have traditionally been seen as belonging within the national borders of states. In many of the African states where vestiges of due process survived beyond the first few years after political independence,[16] the judicial machinery and its personnel, including the legal profession, became increasingly isolated, insular or both.

---

activities, thereby encouraging the investment activities of French firms in francophone Africa. Umbilical ties between common law Africa and Great Britain are sustained through, *inter alia*, scholarship programmes for the training in British universities of lawyers and judges from Commonwealth countries in Africa, specialised vocational and professional training programmes in the United Kingdom, and funding provided by institutions such as the British Council and the Department for International Development. (DFID)

15 Abdelkader Boye, 'The Application of the Rules of International Public Law in Municipal Legal Systems,' in Mohammed Bedjaoui, ed., *International Law: Achievements and Prospects* (Dordrecht: Martinus Nijhoff Pubs, 1995) 289, 294.

16 Colonialism itself was sustained by egregious violations of human rights. It is partly (but only partly) true that the violations of human rights for which post-independence Africa has been famous are traceable to foundations laid during colonialism.

It is appropriate to advert here to the role of the legal profession because of the dominant role of its practitioners, often on both sides – perpetrator and victim – of violations of human rights in Africa. With the exception of the former East African Community, the practice of law and the deployment of the legal process in Africa have been confined within the national boundaries of African states. National laws prescribe and regulate the threshold requirements for attainment of the status of legal practitioner and the duties and privileges pertaining to it. Even where physical proximity made it possible, the historical and political impediments of language and different legal traditions severely limited the possibilities for transboundary movement of legal expertise or legal information for any purpose, including the protection of human rights. One notable exception to this was the exchange of legal expertise through the system of contract judges among the countries of Commonwealth Africa.[17] But informed opinion maintains that the precarious tenure of these contract judges often made them willing tools for excusing violations and legitimising the dictatorships of the repressive regimes that have dominated the political landscape of much of post-independence Africa.[18]

In a continent where most of the inhabitants are rural dwellers, legal services and resources are still very much concentrated in urban areas. Courts and other recourse institutions are also often located in urban and peri-urban areas.[19] These two factors, set within the context of the notoriously poor and expensive transportation facilities in Africa, severely constrain access to legal support and services for the protection of human rights. In addition, the costs of quality legal service are notoriously beyond the reach of most victims of human rights violations. Given the fact that the state remains the dominant economic (as well as political) actor in Africa, commercial pressures and the natural instinct for self-preservation also dictate that only the most courageous (or foolhardy) of legal practitioners[20] can afford to be oblivious to the consequences of fighting in the corner or on behalf of perceived opponents of existing regimes.

These factors explain, at least in part, the emergence and recent growth in the number of non-governmental initiatives for the defence of human rights in Africa. However, these initiatives that define their objectives in terms of internationally recognised sources of human rights norms have not

---

17 Contract judges are nationals of one country who are appointed as judges in another under a personal contract of employment.

18 *The Kenya Jurist,* Quarterly Newsletter of the International Commission of Jurists, Kenya Section, 5:1 (1995) at 18, reports a reduction in the number of contract judges. In 1995, one of the seven members of the Court of Appeal (Kenya's apex court) and five of the 28 High Court judges were on contract. The Chief Justice was also said to be on contract, having passed the retirement age of 70.

19 See, e.g., Chuma Himonga and Chaloka Beyani, 'Access to Legal Education and the Legal Profession in Zambia,' in Dhavan, Kibble & Twining, *Access to Legal Education and the Legal Profession* (London: Butterworths/Commonwealth Legal Education Association, 1989), 234, 240; see also Reg Austin, 'Access to Legal Education and the Legal Profession in Zimbabwe,' in Dhavan, Kibble & Twining, op. cit at 256.

20 The expression 'legal practitioner' is used here as a convenient designation for any person legally

significantly altered the inefficiency of the legal machinery or the indifference of large segments of the organised legal profession to facilitate the legal protection of human rights. The major reason for this is that NGOs themselves operate within severe operational and attitudinal constraints created by the existing infrastructures and historically modulated perceptions of the states in which they are located. These constraints include limited resources; the lack of qualified personnel and skills; limited and in some cases outdated or non-functioning communications facilities; and legal limitations on the registration and activities of NGOs. With respect to the legal protection of human rights in particular, it appears that NGOs in common law countries have wider latitude for using the law to protect rights than their counterparts in civil law countries. In contrast to the common law countries,[21] NGOs in civil law countries lack standing to initiate legal action. Thus, NGOs that began as initiatives to protect human rights through the legal process often discover that the social, economic and political context in which they operate renders it impossible for them to fulfil this mandate without addressing wider and more fundamental social, structural and infrastructural inequities.

However, the context for the protection of human rights through law in Africa is changing. The political constraints created by the Cold War are receding. At the national level, a new generation of constitutions containing bills of rights has come into force in many countries within the last decade. Other countries that already had bills of rights, have recently adopted much improved constitutional texts with stronger enforcement mechanisms. Although it is much too early to claim that a culture of constitutionalism has now taken root in Africa, there is, nevertheless, a discernible trend toward lower tolerance for repression and arbitrariness. At the supranational level, most African states have ratified the major international human rights instruments, admittedly with varying degrees of sincerity. African human rights advocates and NGOs are beginning to organise meaningfully around the institution of the African Commission on Human and Peoples' Rights.[22] The twice-yearly ordinary sessions of the Commission now provide regular opportunities for both formal and informal contacts and exchanges among African groups and individuals seeking to protect human rights through law. For the first time, the Commission's practice of considering and

---

qualified and admitted to practice law in a national jurisdiction, regardless of how that individual is described or identified nationally.

21 Cf. *R. v. Secretary of State for Foreign Affairs, ex parte World Development Movement Ltd.*, [1994] 4 Law Reports of the Commonwealth, 198.

22 See, International Commission of Jurists, *The Participation of Non-Governmental Organizations in the Work of the African Commission on Human and Peoples' Rights: A Compilation of Basic Documents*, 1991-1996 (Geneva, Switzerland, 1996).

23 For an example of how it is possible for judges to use the Commission, see, e.g., *Registered Trustees of the Constitutional Rights Project v. President of the Federal Republic of Nigeria*, suit no. M/102/93, judgment of the High Court of Lagos of 5 May 1993, in which the Court issued an order restraining the government from taking any steps that would prejudice the outcome of a communication that was pending before the African Commission.

communicating information on violations of human rights by African governments provides the victim, advocate or judge[23] seeking to redress violations municipally with a unique enforcement tool in the form of human rights jurisprudence that cannot easily be dismissed as non-African and therefore as lacking legitimacy.[24]

Beyond these factors, the manifold possibilities for instant communication created by the availability of computer technology and the Internet provide opportunities and challenges for a potentially rich and rewarding exchange of information, expertise and solidarity between and among individuals and groups working to promote human rights through law in Africa.

At the governmental level, regional integration initiatives among African states are breaking out of the historically defined colonial symmetry and articulating frameworks that seek to take advantage of the fullest potential of modern information and telecommunications technologies.[25] Thus, African governments have committed themselves under the Treaty of Abuja Establishing the African Economic Community (1991), inter alia, to 'promote the integration of transport and communications infrastructure' and 'harmonise progressively their rules and regulations relating to transport and communications.'[26] In another provision of the Treaty, they also commit themselves to 'strengthen co-operation among themselves in the field of education and training and co-ordinate and harmonise their policies in this field for the purpose of training persons capable of fostering the changes necessary for enhancing social progress and the development of the Continent.'[27] To this end, they undertake, inter alia, to 'prepare, co-ordinate and harmonise joint training programmes with a view to adapting them to development needs thereby ensuring progressively self-sufficiency in skilled personnel,' and to 'promote the systematic exchange of experience and information on education policy and planning.'[28] Similarly, member states of ECOWAS (Economic Community of West African States), which is arguably the most advanced and diverse regional co-operation arrangement on the continent, 'undertake to co-operate in judicial and legal matters with a view to harmonising their judicial and legal systems.'[29] They also undertake 'to co-operate with a view to mobilising the various sections of the population and ensuring their effective integration and involvement in the social development of the region.' For this purpose, they agree 'to

---

24 For an assessment of the evolving jurisprudence of the African Commission on Human and Peoples' Rights so far, see Chidi Anselm Odinkalu, 'The Individual Complaints Procedure of the African Commission on Human and Peoples' Rights: A Preliminary Assessment', 8:2 *Transnational Law and Contemporary Problems* (1998), 359-404.

25 For instance, with the admission in September 1997 of the Democratic Republic of the Congo (formerly Zaire), the 12-member Southern African Development Co-operation (SADC) now includes countries with English, French and Portuguese as their official language, as does the 16-member Economic Community of West African States (ECOWAS).

26 Art. 61(1)(a) & (c).

27 Art. 68(1).

encourage the exchange of experiences and information on literacy, professional training and employment.'[30]

At present, the state is the primary perpetrator of rights violations in Africa as well as the dominant guarantor of recourse mechanisms. However, other prominent violators of human rights are now being recognised by international human rights law. These include individuals, non-state belligerents in armed conflict, and multinational corporations (MNCs). Even more than the states, MNCs have a unique ability to transcend the boundaries of particular legal systems in their operations and in the results of such operations (which often include violations of human rights). With their apparently limitless resources, MNCs can easily overwhelm the abilities of individual victims, national NGOs or even national legal systems to hold them accountable.

As a result of the increasing trend toward regional co-operation, the increased visibility, power and adaptability of MNCs, and the consequences of conflicts, human rights advocates in Africa must now confront transboundary violations of human rights. These developments challenge nongovernmental actors in the field of human rights to build intra-African solidarity and co-operation. The future of the effective protection of human rights on the continent lies in co-operation not only among African nongovernmental actors themselves, but also between these nongovernmental actors on the one hand and the institutions of the state (including intergovernmental institutions) on the other. The legal protection of human rights emphasises the acquisition and deployment of skills required for this kind of co-operation.

Training for the Legal Protection of Human Rights in Africa

It bears repeating that the objective of the project, and of this report in particular, is to explore and inspire transboundary co-operation in the protection of human rights through law in Africa. The Working Group sought information on training facilities, institutions and programmes available to judges, magistrates, advocates and activists. Issues which we addressed in

---

28 Art. 68(1)(c) & 68(1)(d).

29 Revised Treaty of ECOWAS, Art. 55 (1993).

30 Ibid. Art. 59(1) & 59(2)(a).

our inquiries, reported on below, include the content, regularity or frequency, funding, control and overall adequacy of such programmes.

Training for the Judiciary

To appreciate the description of judicial training given below, we consider it important to provide a brief rationale in human rights terms for appropriate judicial training and background information on the nature of judicial office in civil and common law legal systems in Africa.

The Nature of the Judicial Office in Civil and Common Law Africa

In both the civil and common law systems, the judiciary is one of the principal organs of the state, the others being the executive and the legislature. The conception and constitutional expression of the judiciary are different in the two systems. In civil law legal systems, the expression *autorité judiciaire* (judicial authority) is used in preference to the term *pouvoir judiciaire* (judicial power) used in common law legal systems. The difference between these two concepts is to be found in the source of the powers exercised by the judiciary. In civil law, the expression *pouvoir* (power) is used to describe the attributes of an organ of state that derives its legitimacy directly from the people through elections. It is thus applicable to the executive and legislative arms of government. On the other hand, the judiciary derives its powers from the constitution alone and as such is said to have *autorité* (authority) instead of *pouvoir* (power).[31] One consequence of this is that, in principle, in civil law systems the constitution insulates judicial authority from outside interference. As a result, judgeship is a profession to which, like any other profession, persons are certified following a course of training and learning. By contrast, in the common law legal systems where no such doctrinal differences appear to exist between the nature of the powers of the judicial and other branches of government, judicial independence is sought to be achieved by a combination of both constitutional safeguards, and the experience and integrity of persons appointed to the Bench. Thus judges are drawn from the ranks of practising lawyers and no special preparation besides experience and seniority is necessary.

---

31 See René Carré de Malberg, *Contribution à la Théorie Générale de l'Etat* (1920) (2 volumes.).

Judicial Training as an Attribute of Judicial Independence

The attribute of independence is a prerequisite for any institution endowed with the power to redress, subject to appropriate procedures, violations of human rights that may be brought to its attention. Independence in this context comprises structural, institutional, material, psychological and technical elements. In the structural/institutional sense, independence means the freedom of the institution from overbearing executive or other control. Materially, persons wielding the authority of the institutions concerned should have secure tenure and reasonable conditions of service, to insulate them from potential temptations to participate in misuse of their powers or of the procedures of the institution. Psychological independence entails at least minimal confidence in the judicial process by the judicial official and an appreciation of the ethical responsibilities inherent in being a judicial official.[32] Technically-and this is a point that is not always made about the independence of recourse institutions generally-the persons who are appointed to wield the powers of the institution should receive training commensurate with the responsibilities and powers conferred upon them. On this subject, Article 10 of the United Nations Basic Principles on the Independence of the Judiciary[33] requires that '[p]ersons selected for judicial office shall be individuals of integrity and ability *with appropriate training or qualifications in law.*' (Emphasis added)

This last element was considered by the African Commission on Human and Peoples' Rights in one of its earliest decisions, in the case of *Krishna Achutan on behalf of Aleke Banda & Amnesty International on behalf of Orton and Vera Chirwa v. Malawi.*[34] The background to this case is that Orton Chirwa, a prominent political figure in Malawi, and Vera Chirwa, his wife and the first female legal practitioner in that country, were allegedly abducted by the Malawi security forces from Zambia in 1981. Subsequently, following a trial in which they were denied legal representation and an adequate defence, Orton and Vera Chirwa were sentenced to death for treason by the 'Southern Regional Traditional Court.' The regime of President Kamuzu Banda had stripped the regular courts of jurisdiction in such cases and transferred jurisdiction to the traditional courts, which were more amenable to political pressure. The sentence of the Traditional Court was upheld by the 'National Traditional Appeals Court,' but President Banda commuted it to life terms, apparently as a result of international pressure.

---

32 There is a saying in French that, '*Il est plus facile d'être un juge indépendant que d'avoir une justice indépendante*' (It is easier to be an independent judge than to have independent justice).

33 Adopted by the seventh United Nations Congress on the Prevention of Crime and Treatment of Offenders, Milan, 26 Aug.-6 Sept. 1985, and endorsed by U.N. General Assembly Resolutions 40/32 (29 Nov. 1985) and 40/146 (13 Dec. 1985).

34 Communications 64/92, 68/92 and 78/92, decided at the 16th Ordinary Session of the African Commission on Human and Peoples' Rights, Banjul, the Gambia, Oct./Nov. 1994, paras 40-41.

One of the arguments before the Commission in this case was that the original trial was invalid because it violated the fair trial guarantees of Article 7 of the African Charter on Human and Peoples' Rights. In support of this position, it was disclosed that judges in the traditional courts of Malawi, who convicted and sentenced the Chirwas, were not required to have legal training of any sort, and in fact, did not have any. These courts were not bound by any rules of procedure or evidence, and their members could be removed at the whim of the President of Malawi. In upholding the judgment against Malawi in this case, the Commission declared that:

> Under Articles 7(1)(a) and (c) of the African Charter, individuals have a right to be tried not only by a court that is impartial but also one that is competent. Although Article 26[35] does not explicitly state the requirement that States should ensure that courts are competent, this follows from the articles and spirit of the Charter. To fail to ensure that judges have legal training and that rules of evidence are applied illustrates that the government has neglected its duty to provide courts that are of a sufficient competence to satisfy Article 26 of the Charter.[36]

These views of the Commission establish that the guarantee of due process as a human right includes equipping the appropriate institutions of state with the technical capacity and means to exercise their functions effectively, especially in terms of training and information.[37]

Development of Judicial Training in Africa

Attitudes to judicial training vary from country to country and between the different legal traditions as well. In the common law countries of Africa, judicial training is a very recent development. One point of view is that 'members of the judiciary, both from superior and inferior courts of record, are men and women of sound learning.... We are conscious of the independence of the judiciary, as each court or tribunal is established by law and constituted in such a manner as to secure its independence and impartiality.'[38] The perception, deeply held in many jurisdictions, is that 'training' may undermine public confidence in the judiciary, if not the confidence of judges and magistrates in themselves.

---

35 Article 26 of the African Charter provides that 'States parties to the present Charter shall have the duty to guarantee the independence of the courts and shall allow the establishment and improvement of appropriate national institutions entrusted with the promotion and protection of the rights and freedoms guaranteed by the present Charter.'

36 *Supra* n.33, paras 40-41.

37 Access to up-to-date and relevant information is necessarily part of training.

38 Adenekan Ademola, 'From Continuing Education to a National Judicial Institute,' *Commonwealth Lawyer* (Mar. 1993), 29, 31.

During the colonial era, the judges of the former French African colonial territories were trained at the *Ecole Nationale de la France d'Outre Mer* (ENFOM) in Paris which, in 1959, became the *Institut des Hautes Etudes d'Outre-Mer* (IHEOM). Since Independence, judicial training in these countries has evolved in three phases. The first phase lasted from Independence until roughly 1970 during which judicial training continued to take place almost exclusively in France. As a result of the dearth of qualified and skilled personnel, judgeships during this period were open to individuals who were not necessarily very highly qualified. Candidates for judicial positions were first sent for a two-year training to the *Institut International d'Administration Publique* (IIAP) in Paris, the successor to the IHEOM. After this, those considered suitable for judicial office proceeded for further training to the *Ecole Nationale de la Magistrature* (ENM) in France where they were trained in the techniques, norms and methods of French law, culture and administration. After this, they returned to become judges. Between 1970 and 1990, however, many states in francophone Africa opened their own *Ecoles Nationales d'Administration et de Magistrature* (ENAM), which were charged with preparing candidates to become magistrates. Some of these schools, such as the ones in Senegal and Burkina Faso, served more than one country. The training was mostly theoretical, although limited efforts were made to adapt it to African reality. During the third phase, which began around 1990, the magistracy divisions of ENAM were transformed into independent *Centres de Formation Judiciaire* (CFJ) (Centers for Judicial Training), where the training of judges has become more professional and focused.[39]

Within the framework of the OHADA Treaty,[40] the *Ecole Régionale Supérieure de la Magistrature* (Higher Regional School for the Magistracy), based in Cotonou, Benin, functions as a regional institute for the training of judges and officers of the judiciary (such as advocates, registrars, etc.) from francophone African countries in matters of private law.

In the common law countries, English judges, many of them under contract, mostly occupied judicial positions in the period following independence. Judicial positions have been mostly indigenised in the common law countries and, in the increasingly limited cases where countries have found it necessary to hire judges on contract, they have

---

39 For instance, in Senegal and Burkina Faso the CFJ routinely offers annual seminars on human rights issues.

40 See *supra* note 13.

mostly retained the services of judges from other African countries.

The consensus of practice is that all countries require some form of professional qualification or basic training for persons appointed to judicial positions. The depth and quality of the training depend on the structure of the court system or the level of judicial authority to be wielded by the individual. Regardless of the legal system or their judicial background, senior judges are generally required to have a university degree in law and a substantial period of post-qualification experience, the length and duration of which vary from place to place and with the level of judicial authority to which the person is appointed in the national judicial hierarchy. In the common law countries however, no special course of training besides experience and seniority at the Bar is required for appointment to a judicial position.

Threshold Training and Qualifications

In most civil law jurisdictions, the designation *'magistrat'* describes those who wield judicial or prosecutorial authority. A prosecutor is known as a *'procureur'* in French. In everyday usage, the judge sitting in a judicial capacity is sometime referred to as a *'magistrat assis'* (literally translated as a 'sitting judge') in contradistinction to the prosecutor, who is referred to as a *'magistrat debout'* ('standing judge'). In Senegal, for instance, those recruited as prospective judges are required to have different levels of experience, depending on whether they are practising lawyers (ten years), law professors or officials already serving in some judicial capacity at the Court of Cassation (three years), or have previous judicial experience as a deputy *magistrat* (six years). An individual may also be appointed a *magistrat* after completing a two-year training programme at the *Centre National de Formation Judiciaire* (CNFJ) (National Centre for Judicial Training) and obtaining a diploma called a *'Brevet du Centre.'* In Morocco, judges are recruited by means of a competition, which is then followed by a period of training, academic instruction and practical internship in the courts, penitentiary institutions, and prefectures.

In countries like Nigeria and Sudan, whose judicial systems include distinct judicial competence in Islamic law, the judges who apply *Shari'a* (Islamic law) are required to possess threshold qualifications in Islamic law. For instance, in Nigeria, the constitution requires the judges of the *Shari'a*

Courts of Appeal to possess a 'recognised qualification in Islamic law,' [41] but it does not specify what this qualification should be. In Sudan, where the distinction between the civil and *Shari'a* courts was strictly maintained until recently, judges in the *Shari'a* courts traditionally are educated at the *Shari'a* division of the University of Khartoum Law School and Omdurman University (both in Sudan) or at Egyptian universities. Civil court judges were trained at the University of Khartoum School of Law (mainstream division) or at overseas institutions. However, with the ascendancy of political Islam under the present regime, many of the judges of the civil division have been purged and replaced with *Shari'a* judges, who are largely ill-equipped to preside over the civil courts independently.

Under the Federal Judicial Administration Establishment Proclamation of Ethiopia, [42] one of the criteria for elevation to the judiciary is 'legal training or acquired adequate legal skill through experience,' but the Proclamation does not prescribe the quality or duration of such training or experience.

In common law jurisdictions, there is a distinction between 'judges' and 'magistrates', with judges considered senior to magistrates. Superior court judges, above the High Court or its equivalent, are appointed from the ranks of professionally qualified and experienced lawyers. Magistrates occupy a low rung in the judicial hierarchy. Many countries have lay magistrates who are not required to have any judicial training. In addition, countries like Botswana, Nigeria and Zimbabwe also have customary courts whose judges are not usually required to possess any training in the legal or judicial processes. In Botswana, for instance, traditional chiefs, who are not legally qualified, exercise criminal jurisdiction in traditional courts referred to as '*Kgotla*,' where they have the authority to impose prison terms of up to four years. In Nigeria, many of the magistrates and customary court judges are without formal training in law. They are mainly retired civil servants regarded as persons of integrity by the community or 'respected members of the society who have attained those educational minimums, comprising amongst them, chiefs and other title holders.' [43] South Africa and Namibia are other examples of jurisdictions employing lay persons as magistrates. However, in Namibia, the Magistrates Courts Act [44] requires magistrates to have passed an examination in law in Namibia or elsewhere which is deemed by the Public Service Commission to reach a satisfactory standard

---

41 S.261(3)(a), Constitution of the Federal Republic of Nigeria 1979.

42 Proclamation No. 24/1996, Federal Negarit Gazeta of the Federal Democratic Republic of Ethiopia, Sect. 8(1)(b), 2nd Year, No. 12 (15 Feb. 1996).

43 See, Joseph Otteh, *Fading Lights of Justice: An Empirical Study of Criminal Justice Administration in Southern Nigeria Customary Courts* (Civil Liberties Organisation, Lagos Nigeria and The Danish Centre for Human Rights, 1995), 101. Also Eze Onyekpere, *Justice for Sale: A Report of (sic) the Administration of Justice in the Magistrates and Customary Courts of Southern Nigeria* (Civil Liberties Organisation, Lagos, 1996), 59-67.

44 Act No. 32§10 (1944).

of professional education for appointment as a magistrate. A person with a diploma from the United Nations Institute for Namibia (located then in Lusaka) was qualified for appointment as a magistrate.

Post-Recruitment Training and Continuing Education

Many respondents appeared reticent about judicial training, described by one judge as 'delicate grounds upon which we must tread softly.'[45] As a result of this perception, it was extremely difficult in some jurisdictions to secure reliable information about judicial training. In Ghana, for instance, it was suggested that the official secrets law covers such information, making any person disclosing it subject to criminal sanctions.

Most jurisdictions organise some form of induction for their judicial officers. In Morocco, newly appointed judges undergo a two-year training programme to prepare them for assumption of judicial office. This course includes five months of study at the National Institute of Judicial Studies, fifteen months of practical experience in the courts, and four months of practical experience in other institutions including prisons. Following this training, they take an examination. If successful, they are nominated for judicial appointment by the *Conseil Supérieur de la Magistrature* (the High Council of the Judiciary). Such a nomination would routinely be confirmed by a royal decree. In Egypt, the National Centre for Judicial Studies, established in 1981, organises threshold induction courses for new judges and assistant prosecutors, as does the CNFJ in Senegal. The course of induction usually includes a period of practical training in the courts and tribunals.

In South Africa and Namibia, structured training is provided only for magistrates and not for judges. The Justice College (South Africa) and the Justice Training Centre (Namibia) offer training. Human rights is now part of the curriculum in both constitutions. In South Africa in particular, this has been the case since 1992. With the adoption of the Interim Constitution of South Africa in 1994, a Directorate of Public Law Training was created at the College, and more time is now devoted to human rights and public law courses and seminars. According to the 1996 annual report of the South African Department of Justice,[46] the College trained 2,241 persons in 1996, including 545 magistrates (nine of whom were from Swaziland) and public prosecutors. In Nigeria, the National Judicial Institute also runs induction

---

45 Ademola, *supra* n. 37, at 33.

46 South African Department of Justice, 1996 Annual Report, 55.

courses for magistrates. Human rights is not a distinct subject of instruction at such courses, although the curriculum includes a discussion of constitutional law and bills of rights.

Most jurisdictions do not offer institutionalised continuing education to the higher judiciary. However, occasionally there are one-off seminars and conferences which judges can attend at their discretion. There are a few exceptions to this. In Egypt, the National Centre for Judicial Studies is empowered to 'prepare and train members of the judiciary to enable them to advance the levels of their technical and professional skills.' The National Judicial Institute in Nigeria organises regular courses of continuing education for superior court judges, in which human rights education is usually prominent.[47] In East Africa, the Secretariat of the Commission for East African Co-operation has concluded arrangements for regional judicial training, resulting in the establishment in 1997 of a judicial school in Lushoto, Tanzania.[48] In all cases, it was unclear whether the judges and magistrates also receive training in modern information technology; however, the unspoken indication was that they did not.

Institutional Responsibility

In most countries, responsibility for judicial training resides with the executive branch. In South Africa and Namibia, the Justice College and the Justice Training Centre respectively are under the control of the Ministry of Justice. These institutions have their own staff but are also able to draw on additional expertise from outside when necessary. Similarly, the CNFJ in Senegal is part of the Ministry of Justice.

In Egypt, the National Centre for Judicial Studies is a statutory body. Its administrative committee is chaired by the Justice Minister but also comprises the Chief Judge of the Court of Cassation, the head of the State Council, general prosecutors, the head of the governmental cases sector, general prosecutors, the manager of administrative prosecution, and the director of the Centre. However, the financial resources of the Centre are channelled through the Justice Ministry, and the faculty is made up of staff from the Centre and current or former judicial officers and law professors. Persons proposed for teaching responsibility at the Centre must be approved by the Administrative Council and ratified by the Justice Minister.

---

47 Ademola, *supra* n. 37.

48 South Africa and Uganda have also initiated judicial training with donor assistance. In Uganda, DANIDA (the Danish International Development Agency) is funding a ten-year Justice Project which includes, inter alia, judicial training. The South African government signed a memorandum of understanding with the Canadian government in September 1996 for assistance in the training of judicial officers over a period of four years.

In Nigeria, the National Judicial Institute is also a statutory body charged by law with responsibility for continuing judicial education. The policy organ of the Institute is its Board of Governors, which is chaired by the Chief Justice of Nigeria. Its membership includes the Justice Minister and 39 other senior judges. The staff of the Institute includes an administrator, who is the chief executive officer, a secretary, a director of studies, a director of research, and a librarian. Both the administrator and the director of studies are required by law to be retired senior judges. The Institute draws its faculty from serving and retired judicial officers and law professors. It is funded independently through federal appropriations and may also raise or receive funds for its activities.

Training for NGO Advocates [49] and Activists

There is no specialised course of training as such in human rights for legal practitioners or lawyers anywhere in Africa. However, a curriculum for a law degree in most African countries would include courses of relevance to human rights such as constitutional law, administrative law, criminal law, criminal procedure and evidence and jurisprudence and legal theory. This section therefore surveys opportunities for training in the legal protection of human rights for NGO activists and advocates - who may or may not be duly qualified lawyers or legal practitioners - within Africa, other than through graduate or undergraduate diploma programmes.

Training workshops and seminars for NGO advocates and activists in Africa, other than academic and/or professional training, are almost always occasional and spasmodic. Exceptions exist, including such examples as the regional training projects being developed by the Arab Institute for Human Rights in Tunis, the Centre for the Study of Human Rights at Columbia University in co-operation with the *Union Inter-Africaine des Droits de l'Homme* (UIDH) (Inter-African Union for Human Rights) in Ouagadougou, Burkina Faso; HURINET-Uganda; and the Faculty of Law of the University of Zimbabwe. The University of Graz (Austria) also organises annual training programmes on the human rights of women in Kampala, Uganda, while the Council for the Development of Social Science Research in Africa (CODESRIA) based in Dakar, Senegal, and Akina Mama Wa Africa, an African women's group based in London, organise

---

49 'Advocate' here is an expression of convenience and refers to people who may not be qualified as lawyers or advocates in the strict legal sense.

annual governance and gender institutes in Dakar and Kampala respectively, which cover aspects of human rights. Recently, the Human Rights Institute of South Africa (HURISA) has begun an annual 'Human Rights Camp' to acquaint young activists from around Africa with one another and with international human rights standards. The duration of the camp is about six weeks and the venue is rotated among African countries.[50] There is an ongoing project to establish an African Institute for Human Rights in Banjul in the Gambia, whose mandate will extend to training national advocates and activists in the use of international, regional and national advocacy procedures.

The most commonly used training formats are seminars/workshops or internships. Internships among African NGOs of any kind are very rare and internships for the transfer of skills in the legal protection of human rights are virtually non-existent. Apart from a few examples of exchange of paralegals, we learned of very few instances of internships involving substantive exchange of legal skills among African NGOs.

An overwhelming majority of the programmes brought to our attention addressed a narrow range of issues, including the international human rights instruments, monitoring and reporting, the human rights of women, and governance and democracy, as well as a wide spectrum of management issues generally referred to as 'capacity building.'[51] None of the training programmes which we assessed specifically address the needs or special skills required for the legal protection of human rights. However, our attention was directed to earlier seminars organised by groups such as the Centre for Human Rights Legal Aid in Egypt; the International Commission of Jurists, Kenya Section; the Civil Liberties Organisation and the Constitutional Rights Project, both in Nigeria; the Legal Assistance Centre in Namibia; and the Legal Resources Centre in South Africa, in which aspects of constitutional rights litigation were discussed. In addition, the network of legal advice and public interest law centres in southern African countries now meets annually to exchange information on strategies. *The Guide to Human Rights Litigation in Nigeria*, which was published in 1994 by the Constitutional Rights Project, is a good example of training resource material developed by a national NGO.

Among the organisations operating within civil law legal systems of

---

50 In 1996, Zimbabwe hosted the camp; Ghana hosted it in 1997.

51 See J. Paul Martin & Kury Cobham, *Human Rights NGOs in Africa: Training and Some Emerging Agenda Items* (New York: Center for the Study of Human Rights, Columbia University, 1997).

Africa, the legal protection of human rights includes work undertaken within the framework of *droit administratif*. This resembles the procedure known in common law systems as 'judicial review,' and is limited to an examination (or re-examination) of (administrative) decision-making only. This is so because the capacity to seek direct enforcement of the constitution is limited and usually restricted to certain governmental institutions named in the constitution. However, organisations such as *Rencontre Africaine pour la Défense des Droits de l'Homme* (RADDHO) in Senegal and UIDH are beginning to develop expertise in the use of international protection procedures, including the procedures of the African Commission on Human and Peoples' Rights. Along with organisations like the Civil Liberties Organisation and the Constitutional Rights Project of Nigeria, these organisations would be well placed to exchange and transmit skills to other African groups interested in using these procedures.

Paralegal training

A paralegal has been described as:

> a community-based person who possesses the basic knowledge of law and its procedures and has the necessary motivation, attitudes and skills to:
> * conduct educational programmes to bring disadvantaged people to the awareness of their rights;
> * facilitate the development of peoples' organisations to enable them to demand their rights;
> * give advice and help solve basic legal and social welfare problems;
> * assist in securing mediation and reconciliation in matters of dispute;
> * conduct preliminary investigations in cases which need to be referred to a lawyer;
> * assist the lawyer with written statements, required evidence and other information relevant to the case.[52]

---

52 Amy S. Tsanga & Olatokunbo Ige, *A Paralegal Trainer's Manual for Africa* (International Commission of Jurists, Geneva, 1994), 14.

Paralegals are thus relevant to the legal protection of human rights in at least three essential ways. First, they are able to transmit legal and rights literacy and, as such, equip potential, vulnerable or poor victims to defend themselves. Second, they are also able to facilitate access to non-judicial or administrative remedies where these are available. Third, they can participate in investigating and preparing cases which may require judicial forms of protection and enforcement.

Considerable training resources exist in this area which are being actively deployed by several national organisations in Africa. Paralegal training programmes are run by several organisations, including the Legal Assistance Centre in Namibia; the Legal Resources Foundation of Zimbabwe (through the Bulawayo and Harare Legal Projects Centres); the Legal Research and Resources Development Centre in Lagos, Nigeria; *Association pour le Développement des Initiatives Villageoises* (ASSODIV) in Cotonou, Benin; and the *Comité Africain pour le Droit et le Développement* (CADD) and the *Centre d'Informations Juridiques du Réseau Africain pour le Développement Intégré* (CIJ-RADI), both in Dakar, Senegal. Several institutions in South Africa, including the Legal Resources Centre (LRC), the National Institute for Public Interest Law and Research (NIPILAR) and the Legal Education Action Project of the Institute for Criminology of the University of Cape Town, also run training programmes for paralegals. Among the resources that exist in this field, the *Paralegal Trainer's Manual for Africa* published by the International Commission of Jurists (ICJ) in 1994 is particularly useful.

Information on the Legal Protection of Human Rights

The challenge of making international and comparative legal norms accessible belongs as much to the activist or advocate who argues for compliance with them as it does to the state, which ratifies these international norms and is bound to respect constitutional bills of rights. In recognition of this, the Working Group sought information on available facilities for reporting and communicating within Africa developments relevant to the legal process and the legal protection of human rights. In choosing to focus on this topic, the Working Group was addressing the practical difficulties associated with gaining access to information on international and comparative law, which we found to be a widely held explanation for lack of knowledge about international human rights law in many countries in Africa. Abdelkader Boye articulates this problem as follows:

> [T]he practical problems which the municipal judge may encounter in the application of the norms of international law are essentially of two kinds: the first relates to the ability of the municipal judge to gain knowledge of the content and meaning of international public law while the second relates to the scope that is open to him to apply international law in the face of the rules of his own legal system which define his status and role. The difficulties of gaining knowledge of international public law are real. It is, moreover, for this reason that many writers insist on this point which they regard as explaining the unwillingness of municipal courts to take into account a law whose complexity is an inhibiting factor. M. Reuter does not hesitate to state in this connection that 'even if a national court applies international law as it is, in its virginal purity, the law does not just fall from the heavens like snow in winter; it is necessary for someone to do something to guarantee the existence and consistency of that law.'[53] But the entire question is whether this impediment is so insurmountable as to constitute a rule which would release a municipal judge from any obligation to apply the norms of international law when circumstances so require. Such a conclusion seems neither reasonable nor acceptable.[54]

Law Reporting

Law reporting is the name given to the practice of compiling and publishing judicial decisions. This practice is based on the common law doctrine of precedent, which requires judges in subsequent cases to apply prior decisions of higher courts or, with respect to decisions of courts of co-ordinate competence, to respect them except where there are grounds for distinguishing such decisions. In civil law systems the process is in some

---

53 M. Reuter, 'Le Droit international et la place du juge français dans l'ordre constitutionnel,' in *L'application du droit international par le juge français* (Armand Colin, 1972), 19.

54 Boye, *supra* note 14, at 291.

ways more dynamic because the effect of judicial decisions is reflected in lawmaking, in which regular updates of the legal codes are designed to reflect current judicial thinking. However, the interpretation of the law offered by courts such as the *Cour de Cassation, Conseil d'Etat,* and the *Cour Constitutionnelle,* influences the courts below. This section is, therefore, applicable, with necessary modifications, to both civil and common law jurisdictions in Africa.

In the past there were two categories of law reports in Africa. The first category included transboundary, sub-regional or regional reports, publishing judicial decisions from multiple countries. *The African Law Reports* series published by African Law Reports in Oxford, England until 1973, contained decisions from diverse jurisdictions in common law Africa. In East Africa, the *East African Law Reports,* published by Butterworths, collected the decisions of East African courts, including the East African Court of Appeal, which heard appeals from all three countries of the East African Union: Kenya, Tanzania (including Zanzibar) and Uganda. It also encompassed Aden, the Seychelles and Somaliland. The last issue was published in 1975. In West Africa, the *West African Court of Appeal Reports* contained decisions of the West African Court of Appeal and the Judicial Committee of the Privy Council in London from the common law jurisdictions of West Africa. It was published in fifteen volumes between 1932/35 and 1957. The *South African Law Reports* habitually covered (and continue to cover) Zimbabwe and Namibia.[55] The *Mauritius Reports* also included decisions of the courts of the Seychelles until 1936, when the Seychelles began its own law reporting.

In addition to these reporters, each jurisdiction issued its own law reports through its own government printer. However, most law reporters in Africa went out of publication in the mid-1970s. Mauritius has perhaps the longest history of unbroken law reporting in Africa, dating back to the first issue of the *Mauritius Law Reports* in 1861. The only other countries where law reporting has been continuous for any significant period are Nigeria and South Africa, each with a variety of law reports. In South Africa, the *Butterworths Constitutional Law Reports* publishes mostly human rights cases from South African courts, as well as significant decisions from Namibia and Zimbabwe. In Nigeria, the *Nigerian Constitutional Law Reports,*

---

55 It is not entirely clear why decisions from Botswana, Lesotho and Swaziland are not reported in *South African Law Reports.* The legal systems of Lesotho and Swaziland in particular are considerably influenced by developments in South Africa, which also regularly provides senior judges to both countries.

published by Nigerian Law Publications Ltd., went out of print in 1984 after the return of the military to power on 31 December 1983. However, the *Nigerian Weekly Law Reports*, issued by the same publishers, contain all decisions of significance to the protection of human rights law in the country. In addition, in the last two years, the Gambia and Namibia have both begun their own national law reporters. The *Zimbabwe Law Reports* series has recently been updated and is now also available on CD-ROM. The *Namibia Law Reports* will be available on CD-ROM in 1998. It was also reported that the decisions of the courts of Sudan are available in Arabic. In 1998, Tanzania's law reports were updated as far as 1992. These reports are also available on CD-ROM. Uganda is also reportedly in the process of concluding arrangements for the updating of its law reports through Juta Law Publishers based in South Africa.[56]

These are presently the only common law jurisdictions in Africa producing law reports. The result of this state of affairs in countries where there is no law reporting is inconsistency in judicial decision-making. Law reports serve as the judiciary's institutional memory, and thus the judiciary has no institutional memory in countries lacking law reporters. As a result, consistency in judicial decision-making in these situations can only be achieved by 'oral tradition' or happenstance. This undermines the legal protection of human rights and the development of human rights law in Africa. In addition to creating uneven justice in practice, it also undermines the professional development of local or national skills in the use of the legal process.

Besides the few examples of functioning law reports mentioned above, there are other publications issued mostly outside the continent that also report judicial decisions from Africa. These include the *Commonwealth Law Bulletin*, which is published by the Commonwealth Secretariat and contains sections on judicial decisions on constitutional and administrative law (including human rights) from Commonwealth countries, including those in Africa. These are published in paperback and can be obtained from the Secretariat of the Commonwealth in London. The *Law Reports of the Commonwealth*, published by Butterworths in London, and the *Commonwealth Human Rights Law Digest*, now also published by Butterworths for INTERIGHTS, similarly include human rights case law from African countries. Until 1992, *Law Reports of the Commonwealth* was

---

56 In Kenya, the *Nairobi Law Monthly* did attempt to publish court decisions during the late 1980s and early 1990s when it was operative. This periodical is now issued as *African Law* although its coverage continues to be essentially limited to Kenya and East Africa.

issued in three separate annual volumes, specialising in commercial, criminal and constitutional, and administrative law cases respectively. The human rights cases were contained mostly in the criminal and constitutional and administrative law volumes. Since 1993, these have been consolidated and are now issued in four undifferentiated volumes. This has increased the cost of obtaining access to this otherwise invaluable resource and has put it out of reach of most lawyers and advocates in Africa. Also useful is *Butterworths Human Rights Cases*, first issued in 1996, which publishes human rights related judicial decisions from national and international courts and tribunals, including some from Africa.

Although rare, law reports also exist in francophone African countries. In Burkina Faso, for example, there is the *Revue Burkinabée de Droit* which publishes judicial doctrine, decisions and recent legislation. Equivalent publications exist in Guinea (*Bulletin de la Justice Guinéenne*) and in Senegal (*Editions Juridiques Africaine, EDJA*).

For those seeking information on international and regional human rights decisions, the *International Human Rights Reports*, published by the Human Rights Law Centre of the University of Nottingham in England, contains selected decisions of international recourse mechanisms or tribunals, including, since 1995, decisions of the African Commission on Human and Peoples' Rights, and *INTERIGHTS' Bulletin* contains summaries of and commentary on major decisions of international and regional courts and tribunals.

Court Reporting, Records and Archives

Court reporting refers to the documentation of judicial proceedings, including but not limited to judgments. Unlike law reporting, the concern with court reporting is not to assess how these records are published, but rather how they are maintained and stored, in case they are needed in the future for any reason. With a few rare exceptions, records in most courts in Africa are still kept in longhand by the presiding judicial officers. Naturally, the unavailability of faster recording devices increases the length of proceedings. We were told that members of the bench in some countries prefer to retain the present manual recording system because it enables them to control the records, deciding what and what not to record, as they see fit.

The potential negative consequences of the manual recording system were demonstrated by the case of *The Republic v. Mensah-Bonsu and Two Others*,[57] decided by the Supreme Court of Ghana in February 1995. In this case, Mr. Mensah-Bonsu, a lawyer and newspaper columnist, published an article in the Free Press newspaper in Ghana, entitled 'Justice Abban Is a Liar,' in which he accused a judge of the Supreme Court of Ghana, Mr. Justice Abban (presently the Chief Justice of Ghana), of having altered a judgment after it was delivered in court. The background to this was that Mr. Mensah-Bonsu had written and published a letter to the judge accusing him of wrongly attributing a quote to Dr. Busia, a former Prime Minister of Ghana, in his opinion in the case of *New Patriotic Party v. Attorney-General*.[58] Mr. Mensah-Bonsu's view was that after this letter was published, and well after the judgment was delivered in the case, the judge altered the relevant parts of the judgment and substituted a new page that used a different typeface from the rest of the judgment. On these facts, Mr. Mensah-Bonsu was prosecuted for contempt of court and convicted by a 4-3 majority of the Supreme Court of Ghana. However, on the factual question of whether the judge had altered the judgment after it was delivered, the three members of the court who addressed this question agreed that 'an attempt was made to cover up the mistake by hurriedly typing a corrective page, and substituting it for the original.'[59] There is a consensus among legally trained as well as lay persons in Ghana – as in many other jurisdictions – that this is not a unique instance and that it could have been avoided with better court recording systems.

Court records are kept mostly in paper files. Electronic or computerised record keeping is presently only available in South Africa, Zimbabwe and Namibia. Outside these three countries, there was no evidence in any jurisdiction to suggest that there is systematic archiving of old court records. In some common law jurisdictions such as Kenya and Nigeria, we were told that the preservation of court records through microfilming and imaging would require an amendment to the Archives Act and considerable capital outlay, neither of which was a priority for the authorities.

Libraries and Book Resources

Across Africa court libraries are grossly ill-equipped. In all cases, the best libraries are to be found at the apex court or in academic institutions.

---

57 Civil Motion No. 77/94, decided by the Supreme Court of Ghana, 21 Feb. 1995.

58 Suit no. 18/93, unreported.

59 Per Adade, Justice of the Supreme Court of Ghana, transcript of the judgment at 20.

Courts on the lower rungs of the judicial hierarchy and even superior courts in the provincial cities have either no libraries or sparse book collections often that hardly deserve to be called a library. In most cases, apart from Egypt, Ghana, Nigeria, Senegal and South Africa, library accessions are dominated by overseas legal materials with limited information on domestic law (mostly legislation and law reports where they exist), and much less on comparative (African) materials. In francophone Africa, French co-operation through the PARSJ project[60] provides funds for the acquisition of books and specialised journals for tribunals and judges. The materials available through this facility are materials on French law and legal thinking.

The dearth of domestic and comparative legal information was explained as a consequence of the worsening economic conditions, which makes professional publishing and intellectual research unprofitable for private enterprise. It was suggested that sustainable legally oriented publishing could only be undertaken by private capital and that a viable market for it would only exist in countries, like those mentioned above, with a sizeable professional community and a strong enough economy to support it. In most countries, foreign investors in commercial, professional publishing had divested their holdings or stopped production long ago.

In African countries, with the sole exception of South Africa where the adoption of the new constitution appears to have created a boom market in constitutional and human rights law, most of the publishing relevant to the legal protection of human rights in Africa is now undertaken by academic institutions and NGOs. Some institutions that engage in such publishing include the Legal Research and Resources Centre for Human Rights and the Centre for Human Rights Legal Aid, both in Cairo; the Human Rights and Peace Centre of Makerere University in Kampala, Uganda; the Civil Liberties Organisation and the Constitutional Rights Project, both in Nigeria; the Centre for Applied Legal Studies of the University of Witswatersrand, the Centre for Human Rights at the University of Pretoria, and the Legal Resources Centre, all of which are based in South Africa; and Women in Law and Development in Africa, based in Harare, Zimbabwe. In Namibia, the Legal Assistance Centre publishes the *Namibia Law Reports* with Juta Law Publishers. Similarly, in the Gambia, the African Society for International and Comparative Law started and provided financial and

---

60 See *supra* note 13.

technical support for the publication of the *Gambia Law Reports* in 1995. Until the recent events in the Democratic Republic of the Congo, the *Association Zaïroise de la Défense des Droits de l'Homme* also published a regular legal information bulletin in addition to its usual monitoring reports.

Communicating the Legal Protection of Human Rights

The Working Group also considered it important to find out how information about the legal process and the legal protection of human rights is communicated. The responses we received suggested that all jurisdictions require legislation to be published in a government gazette or bulletin. In Senegal, the organisation *Jurisen* publishes current legislation on CD-ROM, and the *Journal Officiel*, which publishes all legislation, is now available on the Internet.[61]

In jurisdictions with some form of elected government, such as Ghana, Malawi, Namibia and Togo, the government is required to publish legislative proposals in some form before they are tabled before Parliament. All jurisdictions reported the existence of some kind of compilation of applicable legislation, although these were mostly said to be accessible only to legal professionals. Most of the NGOs that we contacted as well as courts sitting outside the capital cities did not possess complete copies of the compilations of legislation applicable within their domestic jurisdiction.

Similarly, national advocates and NGOs seemed mostly unsure of the status of ratification of the international human rights instruments in their territories and of the status of the compliance, monitoring or reporting obligations of their states under them. Most organisations complained that such information was not routinely available from their government departments and that interdepartmental responsibility was also unclear.

The Working Group learnt that in most cases the media do report on legislative proposals. The establishment and growing strength of private electronic and wireless communications systems is opening up new avenues for publicity about legislation and the legal process. In some countries, journalists in the government-owned media (and in some cases, in the

---

61 Address: <www.teleservices.sn>.

independent media as well) face repercussions and reprisals for reporting judicial or other proceedings relating to violations committed by the government. The offence of criminal defamation, inherited in common law jurisdictions from colonial governments, and proceedings in contempt of court were cited as two major sources of censorship of popular journalistic efforts to communicate information about the legal process.

The Internet

There is immense potential for systematically communicating and transmitting information relevant to the legal protection of human rights in Africa through the Internet. Presently, however, this potential is, for numerous reasons, under-utilised. Several African countries, including Cape Verde, Comoros, Libya, Mauritania, São Tomé e Principe, Somalia and Western Sahara, do not presently have Internet access. In most of the countries where Internet access is available the telecommunications infrastructure is still unreliable and expensive, with a significant number of countries averaging well below one telephone line per 1,000 people.[62] At the end of 1997, there was an estimated total of about 129,300 Internet hosts in Africa of which over 122,000 or 94% were located in South Africa.[63] The predominance of outdated copper wire infrastructure limits the capacity of most of Africa's current telecommunications networks to adapt to and optimise the potential of Internet technology. This has cost implications for Internet users because the analogue networks presently maintained by most African countries increase on-line time due to their limited capacity. Therefore, higher charges are incurred in locating and downloading relevant information. Exceptions exist in a few countries in Southern Africa that have a modern, digital telecommunications capacity based on a fibre optic telecommunications network.

Apart from a few countries, such as Mauritius, Namibia, Senegal, South Africa, Uganda, and Zimbabwe, most African countries with Internet access do not have dial-up networks outside the capital cities. The practical effect of this is that current or potential users outside the capitals incur long distance telecommunications charges to the Internet service provider - where available - thereby increasing the costs. In some other countries such as the Sudan, which went on-line in 1997, and Nigeria, with very few

---

62 It was estimated in 1997 that only about twelve million of Africa's population of seven hundred million have access to telecommunications. See 'The Internet: On the Cybermap,' *Africa Confidential* 38:30, 10 Oct. 1997, at 3-4.

63 *Changing Africa, A Human Development Overview* (Africa Policy Information Centre, Background Paper No. 11, August 1998), 13

64 Ibid.

65 The address of the Web site is <http://lii.zamnet.zm:8000/cases/fundrts.html>, provided by the Zambia Legal Information Institute, whose e-mail address is <zamlii@zamnet.zm>. Decisions of the Zambian Supreme Court can also be found at <www.zamnet.zm>.

Internet service providers, the confidentiality of the system is suspect. Moreover, in the context of the legal protection of human rights, with rare exceptions in a few southern African countries, the judiciary in Africa remains largely uninitiated in the availability and use of the Internet. As a result, it is not yet clear whether the judiciary will regard legal information obtained from the Internet as meriting the same level of credibility as, for example, a traditional law report.

In spite of these formidable difficulties, the Internet's potential to facilitate transmission of comparative skills and jurisprudence among African countries should not be under-estimated. Use of the Internet is growing rapidly across the continent and the population of Internet host computers in Africa is estimated to be growing at a rate of 85% annually.[64] In response to the constraints imposed on the use of modern information transmission facilities such as the Internet, there is an established culture in many African countries of frequent, intra-country retransmission of information, which could be invaluable in broadening the use of Internet-accessible material.

At present, on-line information on case law and jurisprudence in countries such as Zambia[65] and South Africa[66] is easily available. The decisions of the Conseil Constitutionnel (Constitutional Council) of Senegal are available on the Internet.[67] There is also a Web site for decisions of the courts of Ghana, although it does not appear to be active at present.[68] In addition to these sites, which contain decisions of national courts and other relevant legal information, there are other on-line facilities that distribute information relevant to the legal protection of human rights in Africa. The most notable of these are the University of Minnesota Human Rights Library On-Line, which has reasonably current information on international mechanisms, including decisions of the African Commission on Human and Peoples' Rights,[69] and the DIANA project at Yale University.[70] The DIANA materials are available in English, French and Arabic. Hypertext links enable users to locate other relevant sites for African materials.

In countries with civil law systems, it was reported that there is easy Internet access, especially to French-language legal information. This facility is provided for academic purposes in most universities in francophone Africa.

---

66 Decisions of the South African Constitutional Court are available at <http://pc72.law.wits.ac.za/>, <gopher://gopher.constitution.org.za>, or at <http://www.law.wits.ac.za/lawreps.html>.

67 Address: <www.teleservices.sn>.

68 Address: <http://www.uta.fi/~csfraw/ghana.html>.

69 This is made available in collaboration with the Human Rights and Peace Centre of Makerere University in Uganda, at: <http:www.umn.edu/nlhome/m212/weissool/humanrig.htm>.

70 Address: <http://www.law.uc.edu.Diana>.

Conclusions and Recommendations

Overcoming Colonial Legacy

One major conclusion drawn from the responses that the Working Group received in the course of preparing this report is that legal protection of human rights in Africa is suffering from a hangover from the colonial era.[71] In many countries, the infrastructure for the legal protection of human rights has not developed beyond what it was at the end of the colonial period. In some countries, the legal infrastructure has deteriorated. For example, in the common law jurisdictions, the law reports that thrived during the colonial era have all but vanished. In general, the dominant attitudes and tendencies are mostly dictated by the legal traditions inherited from the colonial regimes. Sources of law and jurisprudence from the colonial metropolis continue to be quite persuasive, even dominant, in most African states. An exception can be found in some of the lusophone countries (the best example is Mozambique), where conscious efforts appear to have been made to create somewhat autochthonous legal systems following independence.

In most of the states surveyed, there has been a failure to develop the professional skills and consciousness required for the protection of bills of rights, including international instruments for the protection of human rights voluntarily entered into by these states. In Malawi, for instance, legal practitioners from the United Kingdom are often instructed in cases which are considered high profile or difficult because of an apparent belief that they are generally better equipped technically to conduct such cases. In some other states, such as Mauritius and Senegal, professional skills training for judges and lawyers in the service of the government was reportedly obtained exclusively from overseas. Few states have any structured programme for introducing the bench at any level to the implications of these bills of rights. We were unable to find any programmes designed to introduce judicial officers, legal professionals or public servants to the obligations arising from the international instruments entered into by the country concerned. As a result, national systems for the legal protection of human rights sustain and reinforce a dissonance between the international obligations assumed by governments and the norms applicable nationally.

---

71 This is technically not true of the few African countries that were not colonised, such as Egypt, Ethiopia, Liberia and South Africa. Nevertheless, the dominant influences on these legal systems, with the possible exception of Ethiopia, are, for the most part, Western legal systems.

72 International Human Rights Internship Program and Swedish NGO Foundation for Human Rights, *The Status of Human Rights Organisations in Sub-Saharan Africa* (1995), 8.

73 One instance of such co-operation was described in Communication 71/92, *Rencontre Africaine pour la Défense des Droits d'Homme (RADDHO) v. Zambia*, decided by the African Commission in October 1996.

Such attitudes reflect an urgent need to update the infrastructure and skills pertaining to the legal protection of human rights in African countries.

One consequence of the colonial influence on the legal systems of Africa is what we view in some cases as ambivalence toward greater intra-African co-operation and solidarity in this field. There is very little understanding of legal systems across the traditions of common law/civil (romano-germanic) law and the appetite for such understanding among some of our respondents appeared quite limited. The major - and in some cases, the sole - reason for this limited appetite appeared to be the linguistic differences between the legal traditions. If this obstacle can be overcome, most of our respondents appeared to agree that 'there is a great and largely unrealised potential for sharing both strategies and the jurisprudence of human rights litigation across the continent.'[72] The emerging potential of the African Commission on Human and Peoples' Rights as a forum for supranational enforcement of rights in Africa also lends itself to cross-border co-operation among African NGOs.[73]

The challenge here is to devise means to ensure that such exchanges occur not just between legal traditions, such as within the common law or civil law systems, but across these divides and distinctions. Consideration could be given to establishing regional or sub-regional training centres, exchanges or initiatives in this field by a group of interested organisations. Part of such an initiative could include encouraging the various regional integration processes in Africa, such as ECOWAS, SADC and the Commission for Eastern African Co-operation, to include such training in their priority programmes and to allocate resources for it. Deliberate efforts should be made in organising training programmes to invite and engage diverse expertise from different legal traditions. International institutions and organisations supporting internships and exchange programmes for African NGOs and advocates should give added attention to proposals for intra-African exchanges. Consideration should also be given where appropriate to including judicial officers in these exchange and training schemes.

Developing a Skills Base for Legal Protection Work

With very few exceptions,[74] the skills needed to undertake enforcement action to protect human rights through law in Africa generally exist outside

---

In this case, a Senegalese NGO was able to obtain support and evidence from Zambian lawyers and NGOs, as well as from international NGOs.

74 Such as the Legal Assistance Centre in Namibia and the Legal Resources Centre in South Africa, both of which have established specialised constitutional litigation units with staffing complements that easily meet the highest professional standards in these jurisdictions for enforcement of human rights under the constitution. A close parallel exists in the Legal Aid Project of the Law Faculty of the University of Dar-es-Salaam, which draws its expertise primarily from Faculty staff who are also law professors. In Nigeria, staff attorneys from the Civil Liberties Organisation and the Constitutional Rights Project are often deployed in litigation even though they lack the seniority and therefore the authority that is readily available within the local Bar.

the NGOs. One reason for this trend is the lack of sufficient resources to domicile and develop in-house legal skills. Most respondents complained that despite their best efforts, it was much easier to obtain funding for monitoring, campaigning or reporting than it was to secure sustainable funding for enforcement action or legal protection work. It is important to note that, unlike other projects, it is not always possible to state with certainty how long it will take to complete any legal protection initiative. This naturally complicates the budgeting schedules of funders, who therefore seem to prefer to avoid it when they can. Internally, organisations appeared to be wary of the management implications of introducing substantial remuneration differentials between staff engaged in different fields of activity, which they saw as the natural consequence of engaging in-house legal practitioners of substantial seniority or expertise.

At the national level, states should be persuaded to institute a process of skills updating at all levels of the judiciary, including substantial instruction on national bills of rights and international human rights obligations voluntarily assumed by these states. Judicial training schemes which already exist but do not integrate specialised courses and skills in human rights into their curricula should be revised to do so. To ensure their independence, it is important that academic control of the judicial training and studies programmes and administrative control of the institutions charged with implementing such programmes should rest with officers of the judicial arm of government. NGOs with skills in this area should make them available to relevant state agencies. At the NGO level, more exchanges are needed between African NGOs and advocates working for the legal protection of human rights. NGOs should also consider developing information resource packages on sources of technical assistance with respect to international human rights norms for the judiciary in their countries. This can be done in collaboration with the organised legal profession. Training programmes and packages should routinely include instructions on modern communications technology, including the Internet, aimed at the bench in particular and at all interested audiences in general.

Organisations that wish to begin or have already developed legal programmes should give careful attention to various options for engaging a staffing complement of high professional calibre. Where the cost of engaging senior professional staff is considered prohibitive, consideration may be given to establishing a network of independent practitioners to whom the NGO(s) concerned can provide referrals and facilitation through training and information support in the relevant international norms. Nationally, organisations could consider setting up legal defence funds managed by independent trustees as a way of equipping themselves to respond effectively to situations requiring legal protection or enforcement action. Such funds might be used to engage independent professional services in appropriate cases. Institutions and organisations that support human rights organisations in Africa should also favourably consider supporting legal protection work on a sustainable basis. Appropriate contractual and reporting safeguards may need to be devised to take account of the sometimes protracted nature of legal protection cases.

Access to Published and other Information Resources

The dearth of appropriate books and other published resources for professionals and activists desiring to use the law to protect human rights in Africa is a self-evident limitation. Aspects of this problem include the non-availability at affordable rates of legal information and materials, absence of local publishers or organisations capable of publishing such materials, and an absence of national law reports. Apart from the government, NGOs in some countries are now able to mobilise the resources for ensuring that this problem is overcome or, at least substantially minimised.

Active consideration should be given to establishing a sustainable process of gathering, documenting and disseminating judicial decisions and jurisprudence, generated within Africa or of concern to Africa and relevant to the legal protection of human rights, across the boundaries of legal tradition and language. Such a medium should ideally be designed to be accessible in hard copy and ultimately on-line. Options for organising this could be continental, sub-regional or national. The mechanics and logistics of creating and maintaining this structure must be studied more closely. The most pragmatic option in the beginning may be instituting several sub-regional initiatives linked to one another as well as to national organisations, which could act as correspondents for collecting decisions and as distribution outlets for the compiled material.

Consideration could also be given to a pan-African human rights, legal and constitutional journal that would periodically publish updates of national developments. The few publications in Africa that are adaptable for this purpose are currently targeted at academic audiences and may not hold much attraction for the practitioner interested in comparative practice and precedents. Attention should be given to ensuring that publications can be purchased at reasonable cost by national advocates or practitioners. It would also be sensible to ensure that any such process or project be endowed with eventual on-line potential. An effective response to the conclusions above would entail the training and deployment of paralegals and more imaginative use of mechanisms that could be used to protect those rights known as economic, social and cultural rights, including, where they exist, administrative and other non-judicial remedies.

Overcoming Elitism and Addressing Structural Injustice

Human rights defenders, whether or not qualified as legal practitioners, have a self-interest in ensuring that the legitimacy of the law, the legal process and the institutions that implement it do not rest on the say so of lawyers alone. A number of respondents admitted that the legal process in Africa is still perceived as, and in actual fact remains, elitist. It is also mistrusted by the overwhelming majority of the population in most if not all countries. Reasons given for this include the language of the law, which was said to be technical and inaccessible; widespread poverty and illiteracy; and the legacies of a repressive state machinery in the colonial and post-colonial eras. There was a consensus that advocates and NGOs interested or involved in the legal protection of human rights must take it as part of their responsibility to communicate literacy in the law and its processes. In addition, some of our respondents suggested that those involved in using the law to protect human rights should show greater interest in structural injustice by becoming involved in more community-based work and representing victims at the level of the rural community.

The project and process of reforming the law and its processes to make them more friendly to the needs and experiences of the average individual is one that should engage the attention of all human rights defenders and advocates. This kind of reform must be a multi-disciplinary process that engages the experiences, skills and needs of common people and represents them in language or through media that they can access and understand. NGOs need to address the problem of access to justice imaginatively by developing avenues for primary delivery of legal service at the prophylactic level. Community-based dispute management and resolution mechanisms should be integrated into this process. Community-based legal clinics, advice centres and legal literacy schemes could also be deployed using the skills of young people under adequate professional supervision.

Chapter 5

Strategic and Thematic Considerations: Proceedings of the Dakar Conference

L. Muthoni Wanyeki

Introduction

The purpose of this thematic report is to provide a summary of discussions at the Dakar conference on 'The Protection of Human Rights under the Constitutions of Africa' held in December 1997. The discussion is presented in an integrated manner, rather than in chronological order. This better reflects the format of the conference, which was designed to encourage maximum contribution by and interaction among all the participants, instead of formal presentation of papers by a few pre-selected authors.

Participants were drawn from countries selected to represent as far as possible the diversity in Africa of legal systems, religions, languages, political and socio/economic backgrounds. The primary objective was to share the expertise and experience of the more than 80 judges, legal officers, advocates, representatives of non-governmental organisations and individual activists who participated. One of the challenges of the meeting was to overcome the difficulties in communication posed not so much by lack of a common language, as by the difference in legal cultures and experience, especially between those practising under common law and civil law based systems. An important aim was to identify the extent to which there are commonalities in the problems and the solutions, in the resources and the needs, of those operating under such differing circumstances and to determine whether strategies may be shared to address legal protection of human rights more effectively.

The first part of the report covers discussions on issues relating to the legal framework and the various actors involved in legal protection, after which specific issues relating to customary and religious law, and to gender are discussed. Finally, the detailed discussion by working groups of issues raised in the legal protection of three specific rights, chosen as illustrative of civil and political, economic and social and collective rights, is summarised.

Legal Protection of Rights in Africa

The problem of obtaining justice and redress for human rights violations in Africa can create despair, but it can also create the hope for change. Africa is more than the sum of its individual national parts. That, in and of itself, is a challenge as regional diversity can detract from indivisibility and universality.

Lack of respect for the rule of law in general, and legal protection of human rights in particular, are evidenced by the existence of military regimes in some African countries, by widespread impunity, and by the adoption and implementation of structural adjustment programmes in disregard of their impact on human rights. In many countries which have written constitutions, limitation or 'clawback' clauses[1] confer wide powers on governments to severely limit constitutionally entrenched rights. Governments also continue to use a variety of ouster provisions[2] to insulate their extra-constitutional acts in violation of human rights from judicial control. Many other governments justify human rights violations on grounds of preservation of state security which is also not subject to judicial or any other form of accountability or oversight.

Lack of respect for the rule of law is partly also a result of inability to enforce it, often due to procedural and institutional constraints. In some African countries, only very strictly defined arms or officials of government can challenge the constitutionality of acts which violate human rights. In others, instituting such cases depends on fulfilling some procedural conditions which are at the discretion of government officials to refuse arbitrarily. In addition, some categories of right such as economic, social and cultural rights, are either not recognised at all by the constitutions of most African countries or, where recognised, are rendered not justiciable. Moreover, the legal profession in many African countries is not independent, a situation which results in systematic intimidation and persecution of advocates defending human rights cases and the control of the organised Bar and its licensing and disciplinary machinery by governments. There is thus a distortion between international standards by which states are bound and human rights practice in Africa, and between African constitutions and their application.

'We get the rights we fight for and lose the ones we fail to defend.' Human rights are the minimal legal protection required to ensure human dignity. Of concern is the collection of norms regulating the relationships

---

1 A clawback clause is 'one that permits, in normal circumstances, breach of an obligation for a specified number of public reasons.' Strictly speaking, it differs from 'derogation clauses', i.e, 'those which allow suspension or breach of certain obligations in circumstances of war or public emergency.' See Rosalyn Higgins, 'Derogations under Human Rights Treaties', *48 British Yearbook of International Law* (1976-77), 281. A clawback clause is, therefore, one which authorises states in peacetime to regulate or restrict the exercise of a right.

2 An 'ouster clause' is one which prevents (ousts) courts from adjudicating or entertaining suits or other applications about an official act or law or a specified range of official acts or legislation.

among citizens and between citizens and the state.

In cases of human rights violations, by whom and against whom is legal protection needed? In many African countries, the lack of clear separation between the state and religion and between the state and civil society complicates this question. The state, religion and civil society are based in the same communities, but do not have the same interest in or impact on individuals. Human rights violations are committed not only by states, but also by individuals, as is the case with violence against women.

A distinction exists between legal and extralegal protection. Legal protection refers to legal entitlements, not moral claims, but what is legal and what is not? Is only positive law legal? Behind legal protection lies a process leading to a definition of rights. Legal protection may involve parliamentary as well as judicial acts. There is a political context to legal protection. Even where legal protection exists, non-legal factors which could have moral, political or religious dimensions - among others - may influence or affect legal protective measures. The aim should be to ensure legal protection in a practical way. Law can exist, but so must the structures and institutions to enforce it if it is to offer protection. Armed struggles and other extra-legal means of resistance arise from the absence of legal protection. If they are to be meaningful and sustainable, therefore, liberation movements must themselves be accountable for human rights protection, instead of emphasising expediency.

Traditionally, human rights are regarded as protecting individuals and communities from the state. But how can potential victims also become protectors? Throughout history, individuals and their communities have been the protectors of human rights. There is no alternative to potential victims taking human rights into their own hands on their own terms.

However, African human rights workers disseminate information primarily for a Northern public, to generate Northern pressure on African governments. Human rights workers tend to be elitist in their approach and often fail to inspire African communities to break their dependency on outsiders; those tendencies should be resisted and African communities empowered so that human rights workers become more and more redundant.

How then can we build on existing partnerships to break African dependency on foreign initiatives to solve African human rights problems? Breaking dependency means creating accountability, creating support for human rights work, closing the credibility gap between African communities and most human rights activists, and making the approach to human rights relevant to those communities. Most importantly, breaking dependency entails breaking down the barriers to African communities. African communities must come to see human rights as vital to their own existence.

It is the responsibility of Africans themselves to break this dependency. A longer-term strategy is needed, as are clear objectives regarding African engagement with Northern human rights initiatives. Legal protection cannot therefore be considered in isolation, or as sufficient by itself, but must be part of wider strategies. The relationship between human rights activity and other disciplines, such as politics, anthropology and history needs to be appreciated. Communication with the majority on the legal protection of human rights is critical. Human rights education is needed at all levels of African educational systems, and this entails human rights curriculum development appropriate for different audiences and circumstances. This pertains to all the so-called generations of rights and especially to the human rights of women and children.

A culture of constitutionalism and human rights must be built. This process should be incremental and all-pervasive. Such a culture cannot materialise overnight or on its own. Another challenge is the unidirectional flow of legal norms and comparative practices from the outside into Africa. For example, most information on customary law in Africa is most easily available outside Africa. A concerted effort is needed to change that situation, and to seek collectively for solutions.

Finally, the difference in legal access between rural and urban populations needs to be addressed, for example, through the increased use of paralegals.

Defining International Human Rights Norms

Human rights norms can be found in constitutions at the national level and in conventions or treaties at the international level. The application of international human rights norms is complicated by the confusion between the multiplicity of existing norms. It is further compounded by the fact that international human rights law is difficult to make justiciable because it states broad principles, rather than specific ways of implementing those principles. Moreover, it can be difficult to know what international human rights norms are binding in some African countries. For example, in Gabon and Senegal, the judiciary lacks full knowledge of exactly what laws apply because the executive branch does not publish them. However, international treaties that have been ratified by an African state can be identified through the United Nations (UN) if the executive fails to publicise the ratification. The publication and dissemination on a regular basis of the text of every international treaty ratified or acceded to by African governments in languages that African communities can understand is a priority.

The issue is not simply ratification but also implementation. Specific measures of implementation are necessary under both common and civil law systems to ensure domestic enforcement through the provision of adequate and effective remedies for violations of international human rights law. In the common law countries, this usually requires national implementing legislation. For example, the International Labour Organisation (ILO) conventions on various aspects of labour law have mostly not been harmonised with domestic law. In the civil law countries where international treaties usually become operative domestically with ratification, compliance procedures and remedies for violations will have to be evolved. For instance, in Mauritius, which uses both common and civil law systems, for a long time no domestic laws existed to implement the views of the UN Human Rights Committee.[3] In Senegal, to comply with the views of the UN Human Rights Committee calling for compensation for survivors of torture, NGOs applied pressure to the Senegalese government, which subsequently requested its own Human Rights Commission to provide guidelines on how to implement those views.

International Enforcement Mechanisms and Institutions

International mechanisms available for enforcement of human rights in Africa include the UN human rights bodies and regional institutions such as the African Commission on Human and Peoples' Rights.

International mechanisms can be used to place governments under public scrutiny. Ratification of treaties such as the Convention on the Elimination of All Forms of Racial Discrimination (CERD) or the Convention on the Elimination of All Forms of Discrimination Against Women (CEDAW), for example, imposes obligations on states who thereby

---

3   For an account of how this change was brought about, see pp.32-3 *supra*.

become obliged to report on their efforts to implement the provisions of the conventions to the appropriate monitoring bodies. NGOs need to demonstrate, point by point, how national law and policy meet or diverge from these conventions. NGOs are permitted to make parallel reports when states are due to report and can attend these reporting meetings. They can brief the committees and observe the proceedings.

At the end of these sessions, the committees adopt concluding observations to give direction to the state. These observations are useful advocacy tools for NGOs. The public at home often does not know what the UN is doing; therefore, audio or video taping these sessions for public viewing or reporting at home can have an impact. One advantage of using international mechanisms in this way is the opportunity they provide for publicity.

The composition of these committees is, however, problematic. Governments nominate members, and the nominations are political, even though committee members are supposed to be independent experts. NGOs should therefore input into the nomination process.

Apart from the supervisory committees, there are also thematic UN special rapporteurs, for example, on violence against women, to whose work NGOs can usefully contribute or whose intervention they can seek.

Under the African Charter on Human and Peoples' Rights, there is at present a Commission, but no Court, although the establishment of an African Court is in progress. The effectiveness of the African Charter, which includes collective rights of peoples, is reduced by the absence of a Court and by the politicisation of appointments to the Commission. NGOs should support the initiative for an African Court critically, to ensure that the Court is independent and empowered to be effective.

Currently, there are real problems with the African Commission, particularly in terms of its dependency on the OAU. The fact that states make the appointments to international and regional human rights implementing bodies such as the African Commission means that members have tended to represent states more than people, but this is changing. Again, NGOs need to become involved in the nomination process and recommend individual experts on the basis of their competence. One way to do this is to encourage wider membership in the Harare Caucus, the NGO forum of the OAU. Meanwhile, NGOs need to make use of the African Commission to strengthen it. It has handed down some valuable decisions, for example, staying an execution in Nigeria and condemning the expulsion of West Africans from Zambia.

States which have ratified international human rights treaties are responsible for their enforcement. More effective pressure for compliance at the international level is needed, such as follow-up to ensure that states comply with the recommendations of the monitoring bodies for the international treaties to which they are parties. But action must also be taken at national level.

Enforcement of Human Rights at the National Level

Don't ask me whether a country has good laws - ask me whether any law that exists is enforced.' In the Great Lakes, for example, only 20 per cent of judicial decisions are implemented.

Contradictions often exist between a country's constitution and its ordinary laws. Judges can resolve this problem by interpreting ordinary laws according to the spirit of the constitution. In Mozambique, for example, the constitution requires that everyone benefit from the protection of *habeas corpus*. However, military personnel are not supposed to benefit from *habeas corpus* applications because of the existence of a military justice system. The provision preventing military personnel from taking benefit of this protection has been considered by the judges to be inapplicable. Similarly, judges often overlook the requirement that *habeas corpus* applications be signed by a lawyer, given the small number of lawyers in rural areas.

Can judges use international law to 'improve' domestic law? In the Mozambican system, judges are supposed to apply the national laws. However, in cases in which ordinary laws narrow citizens' rights, the international human rights instruments integrated into the constitution can be used to help interpret those laws. Labour laws are being reinterpreted in this manner, particularly in relation to children's rights.

Applying international human rights norms through constitutional provisions poses a challenge, given the lack of awareness about those norms. Knowledge about international human rights law, access to the justice system, and judicial independence are all key components in the enforcement of international human rights law. Some judges will accept citations from international law, but many will not. There is a need for public awareness work on international human rights norms, as, for instance, carried out by NGOs in Nigeria and South Africa, targeted not just at the public but also at the judiciary, magistrates and legal practitioners.

There are no special human rights or constitutional courts in some countries. For example, Ethiopia has no constitutional court, and regular courts cannot hear constitutional issues. The upper parliamentary house, the Federal Council, has the power to make constitutional decisions. The Ethiopian Constitution denies the courts the power of judicial review and creates a quasi-judicial body, the Council of Constitutional Inquiry, to examine constitutional matters and formulate recommendations for approval by the Federal Council.

When constitutional courts do exist, the lack of an independent judiciary poses further problems. Judicial independence is affected by many factors and dealing with one factor alone is thus not sufficient. In addressing the judiciary's lack of independence, it is important to draw attention to the financing of the judiciary, including not only the source of judicial salaries, but also the source of the judiciary's operating budgets. For example, in Nigeria, judicial salaries are paid out of the Consolidated Fund, but the judiciary's operating budget comes from the Ministry of Justice. NGOs should also lobby in relation to judicial appointments, particularly for the offices of Attorney General and Chief Justice.

The fact that many African countries are in transition compounds the difficulty. In Malawi, for example, the administration of justice has been called into question because judicial personnel have been in place since the period of repression. How can the values of judicial personnel be changed after such a transition?

At the domestic level, mechanisms and agencies for enforcement other than courts include national human rights commissions or inter-ministerial committees, public prosecutors and state counsel, mediators, and human rights NGOs. In addition to the courts, quasi-judicial bodies that might offer models for enforcement mechanisms include: the ombuds[wo]man of the Gambia; the national Human Rights Commissions and the Inspector-General of Government in Uganda, responsible for enforcing the leadership code of conduct and investigating alleged abuses of public office. Mali and Senegal have Economic, Social and Cultural Councils, established under the Constitution to play a consultative role in realising these rights. The distinction between and statutory or constitutionalised human rights institutions should be noted. Statutory bodies usually have enforcement powers and security of tenure while non-statutory bodies do not.

Two types of non-judicial remedies - arbitration and facilitation or mediation - should be explored more thoroughly, especially because they may be more empowering for the victim or survivor. Other relevant institutions include: nongovernmental groups, including development NGOs working in direct service provision and advocacy, as well as human rights and legal NGOs engaged in litigation.

Commonalities and Differences between the Civil and Common Law Systems

The differences in the domestic application of international human rights norms between the civil and common law systems do not come from the international human rights norms themselves, but rather from the constitutionally prescribed processes through which those norms are domesticated (that is, enacted into domestic law) and applied. In Africa, both the civil and common law systems are externally derived, imported systems. They are based on the principles of separation of powers and an independent judiciary, and their effectiveness depends on the presence of both. However, a concentration of powers in and a dependency on the executive characterise African states. Complicating the picture is the fact that customary law is also an important source of law in Africa. In these circumstances, the ratification of international human rights treaties is often only a cosmetic gesture.

One difference between the civil and common law systems is that implementation of international treaties under common law requires harmonisation into domestic law, whereas under civil law such treaties, once ratified, are regarded in principle as being domestically applicable. There are exceptions to the common law requirement, however. For example, in Namibia and South Africa, domestication is decreasing in importance because the Constitution in both countries mandates the courts to take account of international human rights norms in interpreting both the Constitution and other laws. In general, the difference between the civil and common law systems is not as strict in southern Africa, where the common law legal systems have been influenced by the Roman-Dutch legal tradition.

The need to domesticate international human rights law in a common law jurisdiction needs to be reduced, if not eliminated, as has happened in Namibia and South Africa. This would have implications for the adoption of other kinds of treaties, for example, trade and investment treaties. In the interim, it is the responsibility of the legal profession to raise popular awareness and create pressure for domestication, as well as full ratification without reservations, and to use international reporting requirements to do so. A state's international obligations stand once ratification has occurred, whether or not the treaty provisions have been domesticated.

There is more scope for judicial lawmaking under common law. The judiciary's role in a civil law system is interpretive. The meaning of jurisprudence in civil law is therefore different. There are generally no law reports, judicial precedents carry less weight, and a civil law system relies more heavily on administrative remedies. However, there is more room for judicial lawmaking in civil law systems than is generally assumed.

Finally, the common law system is 'naturally' more conservative because of the process by which judges are appointed. In a common law system, age, experience and seniority are all factors in judicial appointments. In a civil law jurisdiction, one can train to be a judge and be appointed at a relatively young age. However, the 'natural' conservatism of common law can be altered with political change, as has happened in South Africa.

There is a need for increased information sharing within and between the civil and common law systems, to the potential benefit of both. For example, there is no *habeas corpus* provision in civil law (although exceptions exist, for example in Ethiopia), but the common law remedy of *habeas corpus* is based on the Roman 'produce the free man in court' principle. Can the civil law system refer to Roman-Dutch law as a persuasive if not binding source of law in some instances? And can common law make more use of administrative procedures to speed up the response to certain human rights violations?

Gender and International Human Rights Norms

Domestic laws relating to gender-related human rights issues often do not comply with international human rights standards. For example, domestic violence is hardly ever prosecuted as a crime in many African countries.

When domestic laws do meet international human rights standards, implementation may still be problematic, because law enforcement and judicial personnel tend not to be gender-sensitive. Recently, in Mauritania, for example, a judge refused to hear a case involving violence against women, saying that the matter was purely domestic.

The argument that gender concerns are 'non-African' is reinforced by the fact that there are as yet no specific provisions protecting women in the African Charter. However, the process of developing a Women's Protocol to the African Charter is underway, although it is proving difficult to achieve consensus on some issues being proposed for inclusion in the Protocol.

The lack of integration of women at the grassroots level into prevention and promotion campaigns is also problematic. However, in Mali grassroots women did the preparatory work for the law against polygamy, contrary to the idea that only educated women struggle against polygamy, and this ensured the law's success.

Customary and Religious Law

Both customary and religious law must be taken seriously in Africa. But customary and religious law should be implemented in a manner that does not undermine obligations under international human rights law. Should more than one set of laws be valid, for example, when marriages can take place under three or four different systems? Africa has diverse legal systems and their interpretation is not harmonious, especially in the areas of personal law, including marriage, and inheritance law.

Customary law tends to raise not only legal issues, but social issues as well. More holistic input is needed for any purposeful discussion of customary law, for example from anthropologists and historians. But although customary law is a reality, traditions evolve; customary law is not static and its prevailing interpretation can be progressively challenged so as to meet international human rights and justice standards. This is especially so in the area of violence against women. Often, even where violence against women has been traditionally condoned by customary law, that law also set limits to the violence and provided a family and community process for dealing with those who transgressed them. This can be seen, for example, among the Agikuyu of Kenya.

Positive aspects of customary law, such as the focus on compensation and redress rather than on penalties and punishment and the involvement of the family and the community in reconciling the victim and the perpetrator, should also be encouraged.

These strategies should be adopted because customary law is a reality for the majority of Africans; other strategies must address the negative aspects of customary law. Equality rights, particularly those of women, are weakened by constitutional clauses establishing the superiority of customary law over equality rights in many common law jurisdictions, such as in the Gambia and Kenya. In such instances, the common law repugnancy clause[4] could be used to establish the primacy of international human rights law over customary law when equality rights are violated. The repugnancy clause might be especially useful for women in securing their equality rights. For example, in a Nigerian case that challenged the award of an inheritance to a male family member in the absence of a son, in accordance with Igbo customary law, the judge ruled in favour of the widow on the basis of the repugnancy clause.

In addition, the right to appeal customary law decisions to modern law courts is needed. In such a system, a written body of customary jurisprudence as tested against recognised human rights standards would be developed. Customary law decisions would not be taken as final, but could be appealed through the regular courts within a specific time period.

The Role of NGOs

The concept of state sovereignty circumscribes the extent to and manner in which human rights violations occurring in one state can be addressed by or from another state. Thus, human rights protection implicates questions of jurisdiction. But the promotion and protection of human rights transcends the narrow borders of any country or claims of domestic jurisdiction or state sovereignty based on such borders. African governments should be pressured to challenge problems in other African states. But NGOs should also consider how they can address human rights violations in neighbouring states.

For example, what can NGOs in southern Africa do to influence human rights protection in Mozambique? How can change be effected without

---

4   For meaning of 'repugnancy clause' see p.47, n.6 *supra*.

being seen as a subversive and destabilising force? The government of Nigeria often complains about local NGOs' relationships with northern NGOs. This argument would not apply as easily to relationships with other African NGOs.

NGOs are becoming better at using regional and international mechanisms in their own states; these can also be used in relation to neighboring countries. The International Human Rights Law Group, has sent African human rights workers to different African countries. Their presence can sometimes open doors that are closed to local human rights workers. The East African Law Society, whose members come from Kenya, Tanzania and Uganda, has issued statements criticising the records of other African governments in some serious human rights situations. In North Africa, NGO solidarity is important as a counterbalance to state repression in other countries. These examples provide models for cross-border cooperation to address human rights violations in other countries.

NGOs need to work together more efficiently rather than dispersing their energies. How can NGOs work together, for instance, on concrete actions to meet the challenge of globalisation, particularly with respect to the activities of multinational corporations (MNCs) in our countries? Solidarity is necessary at the international level. Formal alliances through initiatives like the idea of an NGO forum at the OAU level advance this objective.

Often NGOs do not document their experiences in a manner that would benefit other NGOs. In Senegal, for example, four cases have been concluded regarding women's rights, which revealed the need for specific training of medical practitioners and the police, as well as for increased cooperation between them. It is important to take time to identify and document the lessons learned from each experience and to make the lessons known to others.

Creating accord is necessary for survival. African human rights activism, copied from the North, uses a confrontation model, based on the notion that NGOs are and should be watchdogs on governments. Human rights workers are often active in monitoring and protesting human rights violations, but reluctant to engage in dialogue with the administration. But cooperation with governments is needed, without sacrificing independence. Structures need to be created to facilitate this dialogue. For example, the Organisation of Prison Monitors in Senegal provides training for government personnel, including the army and the judiciary, in international human rights instruments.

NGOs must challenge human rights violations using a variety of means, including test cases, public interest litigation, law reform and efforts to gain legal standing. NGOs should work to ensure that all rights are recognised where they currently are not. Where they already are recognised, NGOs should work to make them justiciable, by means of constitutional and legal reform. The timing is favourable because many African countries are currently engaged in the process of constitutional and legal reform. It is important for legal practitioners and human rights organisations to fight for laws with clearly laid out sanctions for breaches of those principles.

Are NGOs the best entities to carry out litigation? Are independent attorneys needed? It would be useful to look at the experience of the Civil Liberties Organisation (CLO) in Nigeria, which is an NGO focusing on litigation. How many human rights cases has it won? Has it been too busy doing other things? Is it important to have NGOs that specialise just in litigation, as is the case with some of the law centers in South Africa and Namibia?

To address the high cost of the legal system, legal aid and resource centers are needed, as well as a body of strong public interest litigators to bring test cases. In the interim, it is generally more economic for human rights NGOs to employ in-house legal practitioners. Employing in-house lawyers also means that legal knowledge and experience are accumulated within the organisation.

The need to create public sympathy for reform agendas is also critical. For example, in Nigeria, NGOs used both research and litigation to advance reform of prison conditions. Following the publication of its report on the Nigerian penal system, *Behind the Wall*, in 1991, the CLO hired a public relations firm to publicise the book's contents. The impact was phenomenal. In response to the campaign, the government finally appointed a committee on prison reform which was a remarkable step for a military dictatorship to take.

Reform agendas should also address NGOs' current lack of standing under law. Constitutional provisions such as those that exist in Uganda (Article 50) are required to protect the rights of human rights defenders.[5]

---

5   Article 50 (2) of the Constitution of Uganda 1995 entitles 'any person or organisation' to institute proceedings in relation to a violation of any of the rights guaranteed thereunder.

Communication and Dissemination

The outcome of cases involving human rights should be widely disseminated both nationally and regionally, for example, by means of regional law reports. The absence of documentation like law reports and law libraries in Africa is linked to the question of cost. Where can jurisprudence from, for instance, the African Commission and the South African Constitutional Court, showing the application of human rights norms in practice, be found? A compilation of texts is needed in a form that is accessible, updated, usable and inexpensive.

New communications technologies are not necessarily the best approach, at least for now, because of the current lack of connectivity. However, this should be kept under review as initiatives exist to increase and support connectivity in Africa. The UN Development Programme (UNDP)'s African Internet Initiative, the UN Economic Commission for Africa (ECA)'s Special Initiative on the Information Society, the Ford Foundation's Connectivity Initiative and the International Development Research Centre (IDRC)'s Acacia Project all provide different forms of funding support for connectivity projects in Africa.

AFRONET has embarked on an Internet project with One World On-line in the United Kingdom. The UN High Commissioner for Refugees has produced a CD-ROM disk of all texts dealing with humanitarian and refugee law, including judicial decisions. Producing a similar disk on human rights law should be considered. Models are also available in the form of existing initiatives on the continent, such as Datacenta's ongoing project to create an on-line database of the laws including legislation and judicial decisions in Ghana, the CODESRIA bulletins and journals, and Inter Press Service's human rights reporting.

Better circulation of legal professionals within the continent would also help to disseminate information on jurisprudence. Initiatives to promote cross-border practice and interaction among professional organisations could be encouraged within the framework of regional integration efforts on the continent and will facilitate rights of audience for lawyers across African borders. This would be especially important where, because of the political situation or the lack of expertise in a certain area, solidarity from lawyers outside the country is required. Guidelines for cross-border human rights work could be developed for this purpose.

Finally, NGOs need to consider how they can use the media better. They can work with media organisations to provide training for the media to improve their human rights coverage. For example, an East and Central African project was designed to link human rights and media groups electronically in order to increase regional information-sharing and campaigning.

Discussion of Strategies to Address Violations of Rights

Civil and Political Rights: Torture and Cruel, Inhuman or Degrading Treatment

Defining Freedom from Torture and Cruel, Inhuman or Degrading Treatment:

The definition of torture in the UN Convention Against Torture and Cruel, Inhuman or Degrading Treatment hinges on three criteria, relating to the perpetrator, the act, and the evidence. The perpetrator is defined solely in terms of the state. This is a problem as private citizens can perpetrate torture. Another question that arises is whether to bring cases of torture against the state or against individual agents of the state?

In Egypt, torture, according to the Egyptian Constitution of 1971, is punishable by up to 25 years in prison. However, the practice continues, perpetrated by the police and prison officials against opposition supporters, suspected Islamists and nationalists. Despite the law, cases are rarely brought against the police. The Convention is written to exclude punishments which are legal domestically. This is a problem in countries where capital and corporal punishment are legal. Although corporal punishment is increasingly considered to violate the prohibition against cruel, inhuman and degrading treatment under the UN Convention Against Torture and Cruel, Inhuman or Degrading Treatment, Egyptian law does not recognise it as such. The Director of Prisons can order corporal punishment of up to 36 strokes of the cane. In the Sudan, the public prosecutor never takes corporal punishment cases to court.

Victims of torture in search of remedies face heavy, often insurmountable obstacles. In Nigeria and Uganda, broad legislation against torture exists. However, it can be difficult to prove torture, especially when inflicted without leaving visible evidence. Even when there are wounds, other persons may be accused of having caused them. The standards and methods proof in torture cases need to be clearer, more precise and more victim friendly. The process of litigating torture cases can take from anything up to ten years. Compensation for torture is rare. Human rights organisations often lack standing to seek justice on behalf of survivors. However, NGOs have begun to organise conferences and training sessions directed at the police and other potential perpetrators.

Obstacles to Achieving Freedom from Torture and Cruel, Inhuman or Degrading Treatment:

How can victims of torture seek justice in the absence of effective constitutional or legal provisions against torture? In the Democratic Republic of the Congo, for example, the constitution is one page long, political directives are given to magistrates, and the courts cannot be claimed to function, as most justice matters are handled by the Ministry of Justice.

In countries with domestic legislation against torture, fear and other psychological barriers on the part of survivors make them reluctant to take cases forward, and the human rights organisations' lack of legal standing limits their ability to provide assistance. Access to justice is also a problem in many countries in which the public prosecutor or the attorney general must pursue cases of torture. In some countries, amnesty laws are in force to protect the security branches of government; in countries where such amnesty laws do not exist, non-state perpetrators are often used to carry out the torture.

Proving torture is difficult, especially when the torture is physical but leaves no marks, or when it is mental, especially in view of the lengthy periods of time that may pass before a survivor can get to court. The high-risk period for torture is the interrogation period between being picked up and being brought before the court for the first time. The practice of lengthy pre-trial or administrative detentions means that survivors can be held until bodily evidence of torture has disappeared. For example, in Gabon, preventive detention can last as long as six months, after which time a judge may extend or renew it.

Few NGOs are specialised in dealing with the army, the police and the prisons, often the key bodies associated with systematic torture. Establishing relations with the security branches of the government is difficult.

Gender and Freedom from Torture and Cruel, Inhuman or Degrading Treatment:

In general, women's rights have not been adequately protected by the prohibition against torture, either internationally or domestically. Domestic violence is generally considered to be a private matter, and often is not punished. Cultural practices, such as female genital mutilation (FGM), are not considered to be torture or cruel, inhuman and degrading treatment. A debate is currently underway on the applicability of the UN Convention against Torture and Other Cruel, Inhuman and Degrading Treatment to harmful traditional practices, including FGM. Some proponents believe that the Convention should apply, especially in the absence of specific protection against FGM, but others disagree. Legislation is needed on gender-specific forms of torture or cruel, inhuman and degrading treatment and for gender-sensitive enforcement of existing legislation.

Laws relating to proof and evidence need to be amended and interpreted in a gender-sensitive fashion, to encourage women to seek redress. The nature of these violations is such that obtaining the necessary evidence is often intrusive.

Strategies for Improving Protection Against Torture and Cruel, Inhuman or Degrading Treatment:

Public opinion must be mobilised against torture through awareness-raising campaigns. The media should be used extensively for this purpose, and all available national mechanisms should be employed. NGOs and legal counsel should take cases forward against individual perpetrators acting on behalf of the state, as well as against the state itself. Regional information exchange on such cases is critical.

Training should be carried out to sensitise the security arms of government, as well as relevant professional sectors likely to come into contact with survivors, such as the medical profession. National advocacy and lobbying should be carried out to create domestic legislation against torture where it does not already exist and to refine such legislation where it does, for example, to extend the prohibition against torture to capital and corporal punishment.

Internationally, the definition and interpretation of torture should be enlarged to include acts by a broader range of perpetrators (including non-state actors) and protection for an expanded range of possible victims (such as the inclusion of rape and domestic violence as human rights violations).

Economic, Social and Cultural Rights:
The Right to Housing

Defining the Right to Housing:

Article 11 of the International Covenant on Economic, Social and Cultural Rights (ICESCR) addresses housing as a right. In addition, the UN Committee on Economic, Social and Cultural Rights, which monitors states parties' compliance with their obligations under the ICESCR, issued General Comment Number 4 on the right to housing in 1994. This General Comment elaborates the right to housing in terms of the availability of material resources, infrastructure, habitability and accessibility.

The right to housing has been developed under international law. The question is whether national legislation addresses housing as a right. If it does, then for whom does it do so? A few national constitutions recognise this right but most do not. Mali, for example, recognises this right but Kenya does not.

Obstacles to Realising the Right to Housing:

Article 2(1) of ICESCR requires only that states take positive steps toward the progressive realisation of the right to housing. Structural adjustment programmes, unaccountable and corrupt governments and bureaucracies have further diminished the capacity of states to comply with their obligations in this respect.

International law does not oblige states to provide housing directly. Rather, it provides direction for state policy, requiring states to create a conducive environment for people to have housing. This implies that citizens should be able to gain access to housing. Even if this right is recognised in national constitutions, are there any benchmarks to gauge the creation of a conducive environment? How much of GDP must a state spend on housing?

Generally speaking, national legislation tends to address housing rights in terms of the rights of owners and tenants, not as a universal right for all individuals. When states do not recognise the rights of individuals to housing, the consequence is that dominant or powerful groups of people or factions are given rights over other individuals. In Mauritania, for example, the housing policy is not well implemented, with civil servants its main beneficiaries. In Senegal, where the right to property is constitutionally recognised, housing is no longer a priority for the state, as a result of structural adjustment programmes. Laws have been passed to reduce rent, but they have not been implemented. Land belongs to the state. In the provinces, anybody can partition off land, but in urban areas, the HLM (low cost housing) scheme no longer exists. Construction is expensive and is now almost impossible for all but the wealthy.

Access to land is limited in most countries. Interest rates charged by African banks are so high that even when land and opportunity are both available, people cannot afford to buy. This is the case in Mozambique. World Bank-funded schemes in Ghana financing real estate development and the privatisation of moribund state housing corporations are meeting the needs of industry and business; they can generally be characterised as irrelevant to the basic needs of the majority of the population.

The right to housing is linked to the need for an adequate and safe environment. When a polluting industry is situated in the midst of a housing estate, the right to housing is compromised. 'Squatters' are also entitled to human rights.

Gender and the Right to Housing:

Access to credit and land is not available to the majority of women. This has a negative impact on women's right to housing. For example, in South Africa, real estate agents often refuse to register houses in women's names.

Customary law also infringes the right of women to housing. For example women in many societies cannot inherit their husband's property. Neither can divorced women keep their homes. These problems are compounded when the marriage is polygamous. For example, in Senegal, Muslim women with access to credit can own houses in their own name. However, most Muslim women do not have access to credit; usually the wife who lived in the husband's house before his death keeps the home. When all the wives lived in the house, it is sold and the widows and children have to fend for themselves. This illustrates the need for harmonisation of customary law with statutory law. The right to housing for women should be linked to the rights of the child, as children are usually in the care of women.

Strategies for Improving Protection of the Right to Housing:

Creative, innovative public interest litigation is needed to increase the justiciability of the right to housing. In court cases, the right to life, which has been interpreted in some decided cases to include the right to live in dignity and thus the right to shelter, may be used as a possible argument to remedy violations of economic, social and cultural rights, because the right to life is justiciable. For example, in Nigeria, cases are being argued on the right to housing using the right to life as a basis. In instances of forcible removals, legal provisions such as the rights to due process and compensation for victims can also be used. National human rights organisations should work to advance the justiciability of the right to housing, along with other administrative and public complaint procedures.

Litigation in this area is difficult as it calls for specialisation and cross-sectoral international networking. Developing cooperative strategies and structures with development NGOs is needed to increase the amount of information and research available on the right to housing as a basis for litigation.

Advocacy for constitutional and legal reform with respect to the right to housing is needed, along with education and training for the judiciary on this right, to combat the prevalent thinking that socio-economic rights are not legally enforceable. This right is also politically sensitive because of the commercial value of land and housing and the consequent potential for corruption, which contributes to reluctance to deal with this issue.

Collective and Cross-Cutting Rights: Freedom from Discrimination

Defining Freedom from Discrimination:
Anti-discrimination provisions in international law protect equality rights on the basis of gender, political beliefs and race, among other characteristics. Sources of international law on equality rights include the UN Convention on the Elimination of all Forms of Racial Discrimination (CERD) and the UN Convention on the Elimination of all Forms of Discrimination against Women (CEDAW). However, protected groups should not be limited to the already enumerated categories. For example, the Canadian model of equality rights legislation lists protected groups and analogous groups, allowing for gradual expansion in the number of protected groups.

Discrimination against racial minorities is widespread. Discrimination is not legal in Mauritania, but people from the south of the country are subject to it in relation to education, administration and every other area of life. The law is old and places emphasis on Arabic, rather than on the Soninké and Wolof languages spoken in southern Mauritania. Muslim law is applied, with judges drawn largely from the Bedouin community. UN recommendations on these issues are never made public or implemented.

Discrimination against refugees is also a growing problem, for example in Senegal. Many NGOs provide services to refugees, but they do not challenge systemic discrimination against them, particularly against political refugees and women and children who are refugees, especially in relation to the economic and social rights of refugees to education and health care.

Discrimination on the basis of religion occurs in many different circumstances. As a result of conflict and the displacement of peoples from their traditional lands to regions with different legal traditions, people are sometimes subject to different - and culturally determined -laws, including criminal offences, which can constitute discrimination. For example, in the Sudan, non-Muslim southerners living in the north are subject to criminal offences under Muslim law for brewing and drinking traditional beer. Family law may vary according to religious and customary belief. For instance, civil laws prohibit polygamy, but Muslim law allows it, while the customary laws of one group allow polyandry. All these systems coexist in the Sudan, creating problems especially when marriages take place across systems. Education about marital rights becomes difficult.

Children can also face discrimination on grounds of illegitimacy. 'Illegitimate' children generally cannot inherit on intestate succession (in the absence of a will). For example, in Nigeria, although discrimination on grounds of status is prohibited by the constitution, attempts to argue for constitutional protection of the inheritance rights of illegitimate children on intestate succession have generally been unsuccessful. Customary law affords greater protection than statutory law in this regard because the colonisers introduced the notion of 'illegitimacy'.

Equal pay for equal work is an equality rights issue, in terms of remuneration and conditions of work for women compared to men and for nationals compared to expatriates. Expatriates working for one oil company in Nigeria earn about 1,345 per cent more than nationals. Expatriate workers enjoy exceptional protection in Senegal as also in Cameroon, as expatriate expertise is always privileged. Evolving international trade law, including new agreements on trade and investment like the proposed

Multilateral Agreement on Investment (MAI)[7], will further entrench and legitimise such inequalities, under the guise of encouraging foreign direct investment. In Senegal, as in many other countries, women often face discrimination in the access to work, through selection processes and training opportunities, especially to administrative decision-making positions.

Access to information is important in a globalised world, particularly with the advent of new communication technologies. This is an equality rights issue for all Africans, along with the ongoing problem of access to the public media, especially for those whose political views diverge from those of the government in power. Discrimination on the basis of language in the public media still exists as well.

Obstacles to Achieving Freedom from Discrimination:
Obstacles exist at three levels: before a right is infringed, during infringement of the right, and after infringement, when redress is sought. These obstacles pertain to the cultural, moral and legal climate, and remedies must address all these dimensions.

Outdated laws on equality rights are an example of an obstacle which arises before the right; this can be seen in the laws relating to 'illegitimacy' described above. Few or no efforts are made to update – through reform or restatement – laws on a regular basis which is one way of resolving the contradictions between equality rights and customary and religious laws. In other instances it is the superiority of customary and religious law over equality rights in many African constitutions which allows for discrimination. In addition, new international agreements on investment and trade, such as the proposed MAI, will impede equality rights.

After the fact, those affected by discrimination are least able to seek redress and lack access to the legal system. Those who provide redress tend to come from dominant groups and do not necessarily understand the issues. Because of their limited financial resources, those affected cannot hire the best lawyers, or often any lawyer at all. Nor can they secure relevant experts to assist in litigation, such as medical professionals. Yet arguing such cases can be complex and defendants are often able to afford the best lawyers and experts.

Protections available at the international level do not exist at the national level in many countries. Another obstacle is that discrimination is often perpetrated by private individuals against other individuals, and not

---

7   The proposed MAI was rejected by the OECD in September 1998 following intense lobbying against it by civil society in the north and in the south. However, proponents of the MAI have now turned their attention to the World Trade Organisation (WTO). The WTO has now established a committee on investment which is to table a draft multilateral agreement on investment later this year. The draft agreement is expected to contain the same provisions as the MAI. Opponents of the draft agreement argue that it will have negative implications for the south, forcing free trade on the south while allowing protectionism in the north.

just by the state against individuals; but international protections are framed in terms of states' obligations. Nevertheless, states have the duty to regulate discrimination perpetrated by private individuals as well as by public actors.

Gender and Freedom from Discrimination:

Constitutional provisions alone are insufficient to protect equality rights, particularly those of women. In general, these provisions overlook discrimination based on gender or they subordinate equality rights to customary or religious law, as in the Gambia and Kenya. Legislation is needed to protect equality rights, for example, in employment laws dealing with access to and rights during employment.

Women face problems in asserting their reproductive and sexual rights. For example, in Senegal, discrimination against the Peulh compounds women's inability to exercise their reproductive and sexual rights in that community. Women are not free to choose their own partners, nor are they able to insist that their partners use condoms. Education is critical, because, for example, FGM as a form of sexual discrimination against women will not be ended by legislation.

Strategies to Enforce the Right to Equal Treatment

Domestically, one legal approach is to pass civil legislation on equality rights, as well as to create statutory institutions to enforce these rights, and then to use the legislation and the institutions to sue for damages. Specialised commissions should be created to deal with equality rights issues outside the courts because discrimination exists in many sectors.

NGOs in such instances can assume advisory roles and responsibility for ensuring that investigations occur, representing those affected in court or before a commission, and bringing class actions against the perpetrators. Another legal approach is to create criminal legislation, under which incitement to discriminate or discrimination against any protected group becomes a crime. This creates the public perception that discrimination is both morally wrong and legally punishable.

Information is critical to enable those who are affected to recognise what is happening to them as discrimination and to seek legal remedies. Public education efforts by the media and NGOs can play an important role in overcoming the problems of perception and access.

Chapter 6

Practical Initiatives for the Future

Lisa Finch and Chidi Anselm Odinkalu

This report highlights the main points raised in a meeting convened in May 1998 at the offices of INTERIGHTS in London to review the Dakar Conference of December 1997 and to discuss follow-up activities. Those attending formed a resource group drawn from participants at the Dakar conference.

The meeting began with a moment's silence observed in memory of Hisham Mubarak, Executive Director and founder of the Centre for Human Rights Legal Aid, Cairo, and a pivotal contributor to the project, who died shortly after returning to Egypt from the Dakar conference in December 1997.

Objectives of the Resource Group Meeting

Feedback from the participants at the Dakar Conference on the Legal Protection of Human Rights Under the National Constitutions of Africa indicated that an overwhelming majority found it both inspiring and informative. Many participants reported that they found the opportunity to build and strengthen links with colleagues in other parts of Africa, especially given the usual linguistic, and common law/civil law divides, most useful. However, there was insufficient time during the Conference for all the participants to explore in detail the kinds of practical issues and initiatives that could be undertaken to advance the momentum created by the project. It was only on the last day of the Conference, and then only partially, that participants really started to address this subject.

The objective of the Resource Group Meeting was, therefore, to identify possible forms of follow-up to the Dakar Conference and to answer, in a practical manner, the question: 'Where do we go from here?' To do this, several related questions must be addressed:

- What can be done to advance the momentum created in Dakar?
- What are others doing that may be relevant to the project?
- Who are the potential partners for such work?
- What methodologies are most effective and can best be used?
- What can we as individuals or groups do?

This report will cover the discussions of the Resource Group, first in reviewing the feedback from the Dakar Conference, including the plans and ideas for follow-up that emerged from the Conference, then discussing certain issues which emerged as of particular importance, and finally identifying selected areas where further work is needed and suggesting how these might proceed.[1]

Overview of the Dakar Conference

Analysis of Written Feedback from the Dakar Conference

Questionnaires were sent to all participants (by fax or post) seeking their feedback on the Conference, their ideas and plans for follow up and on resources or assistance needed to enable them to strengthen legal protection of human rights. From the feedback received, it is clear that those engaged in legal defence of human rights feel a need for support primarily in development of skills and provision of information.

Recommendations as to how skills could be developed were not specific. With respect to information, the priorities are clear. Participants expressed a need for information on comparative law and practice relating to the legal protection of human rights conveyed in simple language - especially information on the applicable law and updates on developments in other jurisdictions - in a manner they can relate to and understand. They also proposed the need for better communication of legal strategies and developments to the media and the community at the local level.

Report on Follow-Up Initiatives

Initiatives deriving inspiration from the Dakar meeting or integrating ideas which were raised at the Conference were reported as follows:

- The European Human Rights Foundation is undertaking training of paralegals in South Africa on international human rights standards.
- The Ethiopian Women's Lawyers Association (EWLA) is beginning a public interest law initiative. In Ethiopia, access to the legal and

---

1   The Resource Group established Task Groups to explore possible avenues of work in those areas, with members drawn from participants at the Dakar conference and with power to coopt others with particular expertise. These Task Groups were intended to complement and act as resources for other initiatives arising from the Conference, as well as, in some instances, to take undertake specific tasks themselves. They were requested to report back to the Dakar conference participants.

governmental process remains a problem. The abilities of both NGOs and the government in this area are presently very limited. For marginalised groups such as women, public interest litigation is of the utmost importance. To advance the search for skills and solutions in this field, EWLA has decided to host a conference on public interest litigation in Ethiopia. Invitees to the conference will be mostly lawyers and advocates from within East Africa, as well as resource persons from other countries in and outside Africa.

- **EWLA** has secured a grant (in conjunction with **AFRONET West Africa**) to set up an exchange of information among African lawyers on developing public interest law strategies.
- In Ghana, work is underway to establish a professional, non-partisan human rights law centre. A colleague from Ghana reported that there is no perception of a middle ground between partisan political action and human rights protection there. Ninety-nine percent of human rights cases are highly publicised and politically inspired or associated. The key 'human rights lawyers' are in the political opposition. He reported that in Ghana there is room for a human rights litigation strategy as long as it is undertaken by an efficient and well-defined organisation, with personnel not directly involved in politics. At the moment, a proposal to study similar human rights law and litigation initiatives around the world is being developed. This involves studying a wealth of available literature on the subject. This study will inform the design of the project in Ghana.
- A group of advocates from Nigeria, Ghana and Kenya who met in Dakar have now set up a network of Human Rights Legal Services (HURI-LAWS) offices to facilitate information and, where relevant, action about human rights law in the three countries;
- Another group of participants at the conference from West Africa is in the process of creating a **West African Law Association (WALA)** to advance cross-border legal information and continuing legal and judicial education in the subregion.
- Although not deriving from the Dakar conference, the model of the **Legal Resources Centre (LRC)** in South Africa was mentioned as a possible model for initiatives elsewhere. After apartheid, several advice centres sprang up, pursuing the objective of broadening access to justice, based on the idea that if law centres are placed within communities, citizens will be able to gain access to justice in places

traditionally deprived of legal services. These community-based law centres are linked to public interest law organisations which provide technical back-up. The LRC provides training workshops for paralegals, sharing expertise on litigation skills and procedures, in communities served by advice centres. Workshops also update participants on developments in the law.

Discussion of Key Issues

Training
Target groups
Potential target groups for training in relation to the protection of human rights under African constitutions include the judiciary, lawyers, paralegals, journalists, activists and law enforcement agents. Priorities amongst these may need to be determined, as well as the question of whether training can best be effected at subregional level, or organised on the basis of legal traditions (common law, Roman-Dutch law, civil law)?

Framing: Overcoming sensitivities associated with the words 'training' and 'human rights'.
The notion of 'human rights' is both sensitive and emotive in many African countries. Judges and lawyers generally tend to find the idea of being 'trained' offensive, especially in common law countries. The idea of 'human rights training' for the judiciary in particular could attract negative reactions in many African countries. It is thus important to pay careful attention to how initiatives for judicial training in the legal protection of human rights are framed and to be more imaginative in considering alternative formats or presentations. The central question is: how do we frame issues in such a way that the constituency is not discouraged before it starts? Will judges respond more positively to invitations to participate in a 'round table discussion' as opposed to a training session?

Training for whom and for what?
Training should be thought of in terms of transmitting skills in the use of processes, procedures and institutions rather than transmitting substantive information. The latter can be done through other communications media.

With respect to NGOs in Africa, considerable money has been, and continues to be spent on organising and developing training seminars, but very little is known about the impact of these seminars or about follow-up to them. Ensuring that there is follow-up to training emerges as a central problem.

With nongovernmental, non-official or independent audiences, it may be beneficial to set up programmes with coherent, multi-sectoral goals, addressing different audiences such as academics, lawyers, activists and journalists together, thus establishing interconnections among categories.

However, a variety of methods and selection processes is called for, depending on the target audience. Thus, members of the judiciary may not respond positively to a programme that requires them to undertake specific activities (e.g., research) as a condition for eligibility. In addition, for judges and government employees, choosing the right time of year for the programme is an important consideration.

Is it too ambitious to think that each country should set up its own judicial centre? Can we explore the possibility of continuing education for judges at regional or subregional levels? There is a need to coordinate efforts in programmes of support for continuing judicial education. For instance, in the training of lawyers, judges and magistrates in Mauritania and Morocco, there is a general neglect of issues which relate to human rights. In Mauritania, judges and magistrates do not necessarily have resources or technical skills. They have very poor knowledge of human rights instruments. There is limited awareness of the existence of international conventions but little or no knowledge of how to use them. Moreover, human rights is a very sensitive issue. What applies to judges applies equally to lawyers.

Who does or can implement training programmes?

There are insufficient specialised centres or institutions for training in the legal protection of human rights in Africa. In a continent of 54 countries with a rich diversity of needs and problems, variety in training concepts, delivery methods and institutions should be encouraged. Where possible, it makes more sense to feed into what is already happening than to try and reinvent the wheel, but there may be a role for new sub-regional or pan-continental networks.

There is an almost total absence of coordination on training projects. Coordinating information and making it accessible to those who need it is always a problem. The quality and frequency of current training schemes should be monitored. Can we consider creating a training information bank/depository of resources? A **directory of resources and groups** that provide training relevant to the legal protection of human rights, as well as the issues on which such training is available, is needed.

In West Africa, two centres may be of particular relevance. The mandate of the **African Centre for Democracy and Human Rights Studies** in Banjul, the Gambia, specifically covers the area of skills support and training, although the Centre has so far conducted few programmes on legal protection of human rights, and there is some lack of continuity in participation, attendance and monitoring/evaluation. A new centre, the **Institute for Human Rights and Development**, also in Banjul, intends to specialise in training activists and advocates in the use of national and international implementation procedures. As a new organisation it may lack experience; collaboration with the Institute may help it to optimise its potential.

Training is an area in which fruitful collaboration can be developed between independent organisations and NGOs on the one hand and universities on the other. For instance, the **Center for Human Rights, University of Pretoria** in South Africa runs a pan-African internship programme for law students. It also organises a **Human Rights Moot Trial Competition**. Can this be extended to practicing advocates and lawyers as well, or should a similar programme be organised elsewhere?

Development of skills needed for work in some areas, such as women's human rights, information technology, or economic and social rights, calls for specialised training. There is capacity for training in these areas by using or adapting the networks already available, for example, **Women in Law and Development in Africa (WiLDAF)**. Similarly, **Rhodes University** in Grahamstown, South Africa, offers a course on information technology which could be adapted to the legal protection of human rights in Africa. **The United Nations Economic Commission for Africa (UNECA)** has revamped its communications programme. It deals with trade and investment and is open to address the legal protection of economic, social and cultural rights.

In most African countries where there is a problem with access to justice, many people depend on advice given by paralegals. Some paralegals are law graduates or have completed the first year of a law degree, and others have some orientation in law, but not all are adequately trained. Because of this, there is a real danger that paralegals could mislead and adversely affect clients. In South Africa there are organisations which dedicate much time to training, providing courses for paralegals lasting several months. One example is community law training in Durban. The **Southern African Legal Aid and Legal Advice NGOs Network (SALALANGO)** has identified this area as a priority and is considering setting up a training programme for paralegals in southern Africa.

In francophone Africa, most countries have a **Centre de Formation Judicielle (CFJ)** (Centre for Judicial Training), which is responsible for the training of judges by judges. In some countries, such as Senegal, there is considerable scope for incorporating human rights into the training programmes of the CFJ, through collaboration with such institutions and their staff. Workshops on human rights for judges do take place in South Africa. Chief justices from the surrounding region are invited to attend, with their expenses paid. If a chief justice attends and learns something, he or she is likely to talk about that experience with colleagues back home. A particular advantage in Southern Africa is the historically based practice of sharing judges (in Botswana, Lesotho, Namibia and South Africa). This lends itself well to the cross-pollination of ideas.

INTERIGHTS has considerable experience in organising colloquia for judges on the domestic application of international human rights norms, at which there is a balance between experienced and younger judges. Many of these colloquia have been organised in Africa, and further regional or sub-regional colloquia could be of value. In this way a trickling down of the experience of senior judges, coupled with the eagerness and dynamism of the younger judges, can be achieved. Enthusiasm is infectious as good judgments are shared and applauded. INTERIGHTS is currently undertaking a review of the effectiveness of these colloquia.

Internships

With respect to internships, the **International Human Rights Internship Program** in Washington DC is increasingly supporting horizontal (South-South) internships and exchanges, especially within Africa and Asia and between both continents. Internships (or professional placement programmes) should be carefully designed to respond to the needs of the beneficiaries (both the person and the organisation). Mechanisms to support and monitor interns after they have completed their programmes are essential.

The **LRC** also has an internship programme, but the places are currently filled mostly by lawyers from the U.S. and Canada. The LRC wishes to encourage the exposure of African law graduates to the realities of southern Africa, but needs funds to ensure that these internships, which are limited as the LRC has only five offices, are open to lawyers from the African continent.

Human rights courses

No training package can be of use universally, but existing syllabi and packages can be adapted to make them sensitive to Africa, to legal protection and to the issues. Within this framework, the following questions are relevant:

- Are there any distance learning/training courses available?
- Are ready-made training packages available?
- How sensitive are such packages to Africa?
- Are they skills-based and relevant to legal training?
- Would the institutions involved be willing to adapt existing packages to make them sensitive to Africa and legal protection?
- Who does or could act as a clearing house/depository for training information?

Evaluation

With reference to the legal protection of human rights, how can training be most effective and produce monitorable results? How can the impact of training in this field be assessed? Such programmes absorb valuable time and are costly, so their value must be carefully considered. Yet the impact can be difficult to show with respect to training courses, where the results are not immediate or easily demonstrable. If donors are to be convinced of the importance of supporting such programmes, they need to be convinced of demonstrable results.

Litigation

Contexts in which litigation is undertaken

Attitudes surrounding litigation differ widely. For some, the most important thing is to get the case to court and to maximise public exposure. The actual result is not the deciding factor. Questions such as determining where and when to litigate need to be considered carefully. In a majority of African countries, two trends are discernible with respect to who is involved in human rights litigation. In most cases, human rights litigation is the province either of idealistic legal professionals or of prominent established lawyers who are often engaged in opposition politics. Human rights litigation must become generationally neutral.

The limitations and assumptions surrounding litigation need to be explored and verified both empirically and theoretically, a process that may entail bringing test cases. For example, does litigation legitimise a bad system that may be beyond repair? Can litigation contribute to instilling human rights into human consciousness? Is it not more effective to tackle the root causes of human rights oppression, rather than the violations? It is also important for lawyers to recognise the importance of combining litigation with other strategies.

To determine whether by litigating we legitimise a bad system, the political context in which litigation is undertaken is relevant. Human rights litigation is thus both country and system-specific. That is, conditions for human rights litigation are not the same in Senegal as in Mauritania or the Sudan. In Senegal, the government is preoccupied with its international image and wishes to be seen by the outside world to be respecting judicial independence. The fact that its own courts find it guilty of perpetrating torture on its own nationals can be very effective. In such a case the embarrassment factor is very strong and international pressure in the event of non-compliance is meaningful. The same may not hold true of the Sudan.

Determination should therefore be made on a case-by-case basis. Although in some countries, litigation could lead to legitimising the system or alienating its protagonists from their primary constituency, in other countries it could be effective in remedying violations and preventing future ones. We were reminded by the experience of some of our colleagues who were in Dakar that the cost of investing in the rule of law can include the possibility of facing treason or criminal defamation, sometimes even risking capital punishment.

Objectives of litigation

Human rights lawyers sometimes need reminding that litigation is just one of many strategies that can be used to enforce human rights. If and when other avenues may bring relief more expediently, they should be used. One example of other strategies open to lawyers is the use of boycotts by lawyers in cases where judges are hostile.

In the context of legal protection of human rights, litigation must have a deliberate strategy and both the objectives and the expected results must be clear from the outset. In this respect, it is important to know one's adversaries and understand what is attainable. As with procedures, obstacles to litigation are system specific. Sometimes, the credible threat of litigation alone is enough to force a settlement.

Litigation is not the exclusive preserve of human rights advocates and lawyers, and links to the wider legal profession are essential. Criminal prosecution or civil proceedings for libel are forms of litigation often used as a means of suppression against victims as well. In such cases, choices of fora or litigation strategies are limited.

Organisations using litigation may be proactive or reactive. Objectives of litigation may include:

- **Developing respect for international law and human rights at the national level:** an important overall concern for human rights activists.
- **Publicity:** the exposure of a compromised system or particular form of conduct in the public domain. Court proceedings are usually public. Journalists can report them, people can attend them, and politicians sometimes react readily to embarrassing judicial proceedings, thus providing an opportunity for policy debate or engagement.

In Senegal, for instance, the mobilisation of public opinion has proven to be an effective strategy on the issue of domestic violence. In one case, a woman was beaten with electric cables for twelve years by her husband, a colonel in the army. A coalition of NGOs assisted her to take the case before the tribunal. The case raised two potential problems: it involved a high-ranking official, and it was the first time a woman had brought such a case. The tribunal found the colonel guilty, fined him and sentenced him to six months in prison. This case generated an outcry of public support and was of great importance to women in Senegal. After the judgment and the hearing of the case in the Court of Appeal, the government was forced to improve its policy toward women. There is now a new law on domestic violence. This case is a good example of a relatively small case having large consequences and setting an important precedent.

Publicity can also, however, have adverse effects on the outcome of a case. An information management strategy is often necessary for optimal effect in litigating human rights. Sometimes, this may require the assistance of professionals in public relations or communications (see section on **Media** below).

- **Law and institutional reform:** Sometimes, the objective may be to highlight a deficiency in law or practice, or the inadequacy of public institutions such as the police or the judiciary.
- **To enhance the legitimacy of the rule of law** and to emphasise that the alternative of violence on the streets is much worse. However, depending on the system, litigation may have the opposite effect, undermining the legitimacy of the rule of law. Can we attack abuses in the legal system without undermining the credibility of the system itself?
- **Breaking stereotypes:** Litigation can have a psychological impact on the community and serve to break down race or gender stereotypes and attitudes.
- **Application of existing remedies** (and review of old ones).
- **Interpretation of laws**
- **Preventing the abuse of (administrative) power** and compelling administrative officials to exercise their powers for the public good.
- **Exhausting domestic legal remedies:** Sometimes a pre-condition for bringing a case before international bodies.

South Africa again provides a good example of strategic litigation. When the Legal Resource Centre (LRC) started twenty years ago, the state regularly used the courts to violate the rights of the people. A proliferation of orders existed to keep people in detention without trial, bail was systematically denied, and the state sued those who criticised it. The LRC intervened, using international human rights instruments to argue cases. It was frequently accused of raising political arguments. The stance adopted was a strict positivist one in which progressive lawyers strenuously used the government's own laws against it. The LRC succeeded in effecting changes in legislation. For example, under the Population Registration Act, every black person had to carry a 'dumb pass,' an identity card which defined and restricted where they could live and travel and provided a system and process of permits for those going outside the defined areas. After a long series of cases the government acknowledged this overt inequality and changed the law so that everybody would have to carry the same identity document.

Funding human rights litigation

The problem of the unaffordability of lawyers' fees in litigation needs to be addressed. Strategies that may be considered include:

- persuading lawyers to provide their services *pro bono*;
- creating and funding human rights litigation projects;
- establishing and fund-raising for a legal defence fund;
- convening of funders to set up a regional defence fund; and
- looking to the private sector and to professional lawyers in private practice.

The traditional sources of funding for human rights initiatives, philanthropic foundations, have generally shied away from supporting legal defence work. Litigators are often unable to point to tangible results within a fixed time. Cases usually last for a long time, with no guarantee of success, and a limit cannot always be set on costs. Donors are therefore often reluctant to commit resources outside the established funding cycles. There is a need to meet with funders to seek ways around this, with the aim, perhaps, of setting up a pool of funds for legal defence either regionally or subregionally.

In addition to international donors, we need to think of ways to draw on national resources wherever possible, for example, from the business community.

NGOs: Legal Capacity and Personnel

To work effectively and responsibly on the constitutional protection of human rights, NGOs need access to those with legal skills and expertise in the legal protection of human rights, whether by employing lawyers directly or by being otherwise able to utilise their services. Effective action by NGOs for the legal protection of human rights depends on well-defined strategies.

In West Africa, the biggest problem with respect to the use, application or enforcement of human rights norms is determining who can do this work within NGOs. In francophone countries, most NGOs do not have legal advisers. A professional lawyer can be assigned to a specific case, but often such lawyers do not know how to apply human rights law. NGOs in South Africa, like the LRC, are finding it difficult to retain good lawyers. Private legal practice and the business and governmental sectors all promise better remuneration and perks; consequently, skilled professionals are being drained from the NGO sector.

Litigation, perhaps more than any other aspect of legal protection work, requires professional and technical skills. Collaboration on individual cases is called for. In francophone countries, NGOs have no capacity to sue or conduct cases in their own name. However, bar associations and private lawyers do have this capacity, hence the need to work with them. Ideally, it helps to be able to use or call on the services of experienced lawyers, although in reality very few NGOs can afford to do so.

Media

The liberalisation of the mainstream media continues, but in order to maximise it as a tool for the promotion of human rights, reporters need to be able to find appropriate stories, write about them from a human rights perspective, and interpret legal issues for lay readers. This requires the acquisition of some specialised skills on their part, which can be facilitated by human rights NGOs and lawyers.

Well-targeted and well-designed regional training sessions on international human rights law for reporters and journalists can help them to develop the necessary skills. NGOs and others can assist by providing very practical information tools designed with journalists' needs in mind so that, as stories surface, journalists can recognise the legal issues involved and the potential links to human rights protection.

Lawyers need to learn how to communicate with NGOs and the media and make legal information more accessible to non-lawyers. This may be an appropriate subject for training programmes.

It is important to conceive of the media broadly. Communication can take multiple forms, among them, theatre, posters, print, and electronic media. An information and communications strategy should clarify the goals of communication in legal cases and determine how these goals can be achieved. Often, selective and appropriate targeting is vital.

Cross-Sectoral Cooperation for the Legal Protection of Human Rights

The political isolation of the human rights movement must be broken down. There is, for instance, an interface between human rights law, humanitarian law and peace and conflict resolution which is not sufficiently used. In practice, expertise from other sectors is often required for effective work in the legal protection of human rights. This is particularly true in relation to cases dealing with the protection of economic and social rights or the environment. Similarly, rights relating to health, such as reproductive health rights or the rights dimension of the AIDS pandemic, inevitably involve cross-sectoral cooperation. Community solidarity and political action can also reinforce legal action. In some countries, this has been particularly useful in the protection of trade union rights.

Groups undertaking action to protect human rights through the law can set up effective liaison among NGOs, legal professionals, and community media groups and networks. In Senegal, for instance, Rencontre Africaine pour la Défense des Droits de l'Homme (RADDHO) has organised several specialised commissions. For example, a medical commission is used to provide technical advice and support in the investigation of torture. Other commissions focus on the judicial system, research and education, and women and children. In order for information to reach communities, civic education networks should be set up and information sharing networks developed.

Significant institutional changes have been taking place within development NGOs. Such organisations are often particularly concerned with the involvement of financial institutions in the design and implementation of governmental policies which in turn have an impact on human rights. Language, a powerful medium, has shifted from using words such as 'basic needs' to 'basic rights'. This is therefore a particularly opportune time to link up with development NGOs.

Tasks and Task Groups

A session of the resource group meeting was devoted to identifying tasks that might be undertaken to guide and stimulate follow up initiatives, defining issues to be addressed and steps to be taken and assigning responsibility for coordinating action.[2]

Conference reports

Two publications will result from the conference. The first will be the conference report, which will contain a summary report on the conference prepared by the conference rapporteur, the overview paper on the country studies, the Working Group (training and information) report, and a report on this meeting of the resource group. This publication is intended primarily for use by activists. It will be produced in a short, easily digestible form, in English, French and Arabic, and will be widely distributed.

---

2   See n.1 above.

The second publication will be a compilation of edited versions of the country studies conducted for the project. It will include the country reports (fully revised and edited), the Working Group paper, and the overview papers from both the common and civil law perspectives. The time frame for this publication will be longer, as it will be published by an established commercial publisher in English, and possibly in French as well. The book will appeal primarily to an academic and legal audience.

Litigation Pilot Project

The purpose of the pilot project is to test the viability of litigation as a tool in several countries and to test programmes to provide support and solidarity to those who undertake this work. Litigation is already a well-established strategy, but the idea is to share expertise, resources and strategies with others, drawing on resources rarely available in any one country. The end product should be a conceptualisation of various forms of litigation-based action in different countries and the forms of training, support, information and communication linkages that may be required. The pilot project would have a limited time frame (e.g., 5 years) but there would be no geographic limitations.

The project should be proactive and strategic in defining litigation tasks and objectives and taking steps to realise them. Potential partner organisations in each country should be invited to provide input into the design of the pilot project. The Task Group should develop a master plan based on consensus among all partners, but which reflects, to some degree, country specificity. Project design and implementation should be able to benefit from the expertise of the Task Group, the partners and the wider team that participated in the Dakar conference.

This is a difficult idea to conceptualise. It marks a shift from the theoretical stage to the practical application stage of the project. It could be conceived as a single project or three separate projects, dealing with litigation, training and information individually. The pilot project should be centred on litigation, with close links to training, communications and other pertinent areas.

Related to the design of the project is determining the type of management structure that will enable project implementation to be as practical as possible. If one entity were to undertake the management and co-ordination of all three components - litigation, training and information

- there is a very real risk that it would be stretched too thin. Different skills are required for each of the three areas. Moreover, litigation is country-specific, while information and training may cross national borders to different degrees. To preserve coherence and coordination, the ideal would be to have a single project, but one in which management responsibilities are shared rather than undertaken by a single entity.

The coordinator of the litigation component of the project could identify, for example, a group in Uganda with a case where there is a good possibility of litigation on the issue but seeking additional expertise. The coordinator would assist in identifying expertise to help develop a strategy and provide necessary resources, drawing on information, experience and expertise from elsewhere in the region. For its part, the local group would maintain control of implementation of the strategy. The overall goal of the pilot project is to provide a pool of expertise into which national actors can tap.

Funding public interest legal defence work in Africa:

The Task Group working in this area should address three objectives:
- define clearly, in consultation with national groups and practitioners, what the needs are in this area;
- taking account of different national contexts, explore how funds can be made available and administered for work in this field; and
- explore the possibility of setting up a meeting of donors to respond to the needs and modalities identified.

Justiciability of economic and social rights

This is a growing area of interest and concern to groups in Africa in particular. The **International Commission of Jurists** recently organised a workshop with the **African Development Bank** on the implementation of economic and social rights in Africa. The **American Association for the Advancement of Science and HURIDOCS** are also working on developing methods for monitoring violations of economic, social and cultural rights. The Task Group will concentrate on ways to develop support for broadening the justiciability of economic and social rights in Africa.

African law centres internship/exchange

Most interns hosted by African organisations come from the USA, Canada, or other Northern countries. There is a paucity of African interns going to other African countries and organisations. Moreover, most internships are oriented toward NGOs and students. There is a special need for law-related human rights internships for Africans, including professional lawyers, but also targetting law students who are about to finish their degrees. A system of exchanges and internships should be established. Ways to finance such visits should also be explored.

An internship programme – the **Africa Law Students Internship Programme** – run by the **Center for Human Rights** at the **University of Pretoria** already exists; it could be approached to see whether it could be expanded to include practicing lawyers. Similarly, the **African Society of International and Comparative Law** has a professional placement programme, which supports the placement of African lawyers at the African Commission on Human and Peoples' Rights for one year. Both organisations (the University of Pretoria Human Rights Centre and the African Society) have worked together in this area and should be asked to contribute their ideas. An internship project would benefit from the assistance of a carefully constituted advisory group.

A Task Group will develop these ideas.

Africa-sensitive information materials

The Task Group working on this aspect will:

- determine the range and scope of materials available;
- explore how best to bring these materials to the attention of those who need access to them in Africa; and
- recommend and possibly initiate contacts with potential sources of such information materials.

Based on the information collected, further needs can be identified and plans for developing appropriate materials devised.

Directories

Directories of individuals and groups active in the legal protection of human rights in Africa, opportunities and initiatives for training in this area, and available resources would be valuable. Such directories could be combined in one all-encompassing directory or be three separate directories. A university or a consortium of universities might be best placed to undertake this work and benefit from it. A Task Group will explore this idea further.

Electronic library
on the legal protection of human rights

The purpose of the electronic library would be to make primary legislation and decisions of national and regional human rights courts and other human rights mechanisms accessible on the Internet. The Task Group will:

• identify existing Internet sites carrying African legal materials;
• identify any other groups in Africa with the capacity for generating or linking to Internet-based or Internet-accessible African legal information; and
• help to generate interest in this project, identifying groups that may be interested in working on it.

Presently, entities like **Datacenta** in Ghana and **Juricen** in Senegal have begun to create electronic libraries of primary legal information in both English- and French-speaking Africa respectively. The **Human Rights and Peace Centre (HURIPEC)** at Makerere University also has considerable Internet-accessible information on international human rights law. In addition, there is also the communication programme at the **UNECA**. The Task Group could try to pool the skills and resources available from these sources.

Newsletter and bulletin on legal
developments relating to human rights in Africa

This can probably best be undertaken by an existing publication. The Task Group will contact journals such as the *Nairobi Law Monthly* in Kenya and the *HURI-LAWS Newsletter* in Nigeria to explore who might be interested in undertaking this initiative.

Contributors

Mr Olisa Agbakoba
Legal Practitioner
Olisa Agbakoba & Associates
Lagos, Nigeria

Professor Abdullahi An Na'im
School of Law
Emory University, USA

Ms Meaza Ashenafi
Executive Director
Ethiopian Women Lawyers Association
Addis Ababa, Ethiopia

Mr Nana Busia
West Africa Programme Manager
International Alert, UK

Professor Abdoullah Cisse
Universite de Saint Louis
Senegal

Ms Shirin Aumeeruddy-Cziffra
Barrister-at-law
Mauritius

Ms Lisa Finch
Programme Assistant
Interights, UK

Mr Michelo Hunsungule
Raoul Wallenberg Institute
Zambia

Mr Siddig Hussein
Lecturer
Faculty of Law
University of Khartoum, Sudan

Mr Ibrahima Kane
Legal Officer, Africa
Interights

Mr A Rahim Khan
Attorney
Rahim Khan & Company
Botswana

Ms Bibiane Mbaye Gahamanyi
Administrateur
Union Pour l'Etude de la Population
Africaine
Senegal

Mr Mwangi Mbuthia
(deceased)
Kenya

Mr Kathurima M'Inoti
International Commission of Jurists
(Kenyan Section)
Kenya

Justice Luis Mondlane
President, Supreme Court of
Mozambique
Mozambique

Mr Hisham Mubarak
(Deceased)
Egypt

Mr Ngande Mwanajiti
Executive Director
AFRONET
Zambia

Professor Abdelaziz Nouaydi
Lecturer in Law
University of Fez
Morocco

Mr Chidi Anselm Odinkalu
Senior Legal Officer
Interights

Ms Emma Playfair
Executive Director
Interights

Mr Amir Salem
Executive Director
Legal Research and Resources Centre for
Human Rights
Cairo, Egypt

Mr Amadou Sakho
Conseiller Juridique
Conakry, Guinea

Mr Livingstone Sewanyana
Excecutive Director
Foundation for Human Rights Initiative
Kampala, Uganda

Ms Lucrecia Seafield
Project Officer
European Foundation for Human Rights
South Africa

Mr Yosias Tadesse
Writer
Ethiopia

Ms Muthoni Lynn Wanyeki
Journalist
Kenya

Ms Gita Welch
UNIFEM
Harare, Zimbabwe

List Of Participants

Ms Christine Achieng
Research Officer
Foundation for Human Rights Initiative
Plot 77, Makerere Hill Road
PO Box 11027
Kampala, Uganda
Tel: + 256 41 530 095
Fax: + 256 41 540 561
Email: FHRI@starcom.co.ug

Mr Olisa Agbakoba
Legal Practitioner
Olisa Agbakoba & Associates
Maritime Complex
34 Creek Road
PO Box 3169, Apapa,
Lagos, Nigeria
Tel: + 234 1 587 67 06
Fax: + 234 1 587 68 76
Email: Olisa@rcl.nig.com
Huri-laws@alpha.linkserve.com

Mrs Veronique Akankossi-Deguenon
Association des Femmes Juristes
BP 01 - 3486
Cotonou, Benin
Tel: + 229 31 49 54
Fax: + 229 32 27 86
Email: afjb.benin@internet.bj

Prof Abdullahi An Na'im
School of Law
Emory University
Atlanta 30322 2770, USA
Tel: + 1 404 727 1198
Fax: + 1 404 727 6820
Email: aannaim@law.emory.edu

Ms Meaza Ashenafi
Executive Director
Ethiopian Women Lawyers Association
PO Box 13760
Addis Ababa, Ethiopia
Tel: + 251 1 51 91 48
Fax: + 251 1 53 18 18
Email: ewla@telecom.net.et

Mr Guillaume Ngefa Atondoko
Advocate
9 rue Richmont apt. 21
Geneva 1202, Switzerland
Tel: + 41 22 731 5713
Email: ngefa@hotmail.com

Ms Taaka Awori
Program Associate
Associates for Change
PO Box 9627
Kampala, Uganda
Tel: + 256 41 342 230
Fax: + 256 41 530 412
Email: Butegwa@starcom.co.ug

Mr Andre Basse
Ministere des Affaires Etrangeres
BP 4044
Dakar, Sénégal
Tel/fax: + 221 823 62 71

Mr Kojo Bentsi-Enchill
Legal Practitioner
Bentsi-Enchill, Letsa & Mate
1st Floor, Teachers' Hall Annex
Adabraka, Accra
Ghana
Tel: + 233 21 22 1191/ 027 554335/028
213145
Fax: + 233 21 226 129/ 220 629
Email: Belm@africaonline.com.gh/
Bentsi@Ghana.com

*Mr Chaloka Beyani
Dept of Law
London School of Economics
Houghton Street,
London, WC2 2AE
UK
Tel: 0171 955 6388
Email: C.BEYANI@LSE.AC.UK

Mr Nana Busia
West Africa Programme Manager
International Alert
1 Glyn Street
London SE115HT,
UK
Tel: + 44 171 793 83 83
Fax: + 44 171 793 79 75
Email: nbusia@international-alert.org

Prof Abdoullah Cisse
Université de Saint Louis
BP 711
Saint Louis, Sénégal
Tel/fax: + 221 961 3552
Email: personnel@metisscana.sn

Ms Shirin Aumeerudy-Cziffra
Barrister-at-Law
210 Chancery House
14 Lislet Geoffrey Street
Port Louis, Mauritius
Tel: + 230 454 65 36
Fax: + 230 211 59 27

Mr Mohammed Dicko
Magistrat
Ecole Regionale Superieure de la
Magistature
02 BP 353
Benin
Tel: + 229 22 58 03
Fax: + 229 22 43 67

Mr Alpha Fall
Director of Programmes
Institute for Human Rights and
Development
PO Box 1896
Banjul, The Gambia
Tel: + 220 496 421
Fax: + 220 494 178
Email: institute@gamtel.gm

Mr Fernando Gomez
President
Guinea Bissau League of Human Rights
BP 599, Bissau
Guinea Bissau
T/Fax: + 245 201 766

Ms Stephanie Grant
Lawyers' Committee for Human Rights
333 Seventh Avenue
13th Floor
New York NY 10001, USA
Tel: + 1 212 845 5245
Fax: + 1 212 845 5299
Grants@LCHR.ORG

Mr Michelo Hansungule
Raoul Wallenberg Institute
Lund University, PO Box 1155
S-221 05 Lund, Sweden
Tel: + 46 46 222 1238
Fax: + 46 46 222 1222

Ms Julia Harrington
Executive Director
Institute for Human Rights and

Development
PO Box 1896
Banjul, The Gambia
Tel: + 220 496 421
Fax: + 220 494 178
Email: institute@gamtel.gm

Mr Siddig Hussein
Lecturer
Faculty of Law
University of Khartoum
PO Box 10738
Khartoum, Sudan
Tel: + 249 12 300672
Fax: + 249 77 1740

Mr A Rahim Khan
Attorney
Rahim Khan & Company
Grnd Floor, Debswana House
PB 1884
Gaborone, Botswana
Tel: + 267 31379/371611
Fax: + 267 313020
Email: sam@info.bw

Mr Zachael Ki
Lecturer
MBDHP
03 BP 7024
Ouagadougou 03
Burkina Faso
Tel: + 226 31 61 45
Fax: + 226 31 61 44

Mr Clinton Light
Attorney
Legal Assistance Centre
PO Box 604
Windhoek, Namibia
Tel: + 264 61 223356
Fax: + 264 61 234953
Email: lac@iwwn.com.na/
legal@iafrica.com.na

*Mr Mathias Marcussen
Legal Adviser
Office of the Prosecutor
International Criminal Tribunal for
Rwanda, PO Box 749
Kigali, Rwanda
Tel: + 255 842 69/+1 212 963 9906
Fax: + 1 212 963 4001

*Dr Maria Mabota
President
Liga Mocambicano dos Direitos
Humanos
Av 24 de Julho 776
R/C Maputo
Mozambique
Tel: + 258 1 423017/430705
Fax: + 258 1 430706

Mr Bongani Majola
Legal Resource Centre
7th Floor
Sable Centre
41 De Korte Street
2001 Braamfontein
South Africa
Email: Bongani@lrc.org.za
Tel: + 27 11 403 76 94
Fax: + 27 11 403 10 58

Ms Margaret Manalula
Faculty of Law
University of Zambia
Lusaka, Zambia
Tel: + 260 1 25 25 14

Ms Dumisani Mashingaidze
National Coordinator
Women and Law in Southern Africa
Research Trust (WLSA)
16 Lawson Avenue
Milton Park, Harare
Zimbabwe
Tel/Fax: + 263 4 793 401
Cell: + 011 405 222

Ms Fatimata Mbaye
Vice Presidente de L'Association des
Droits de l'Homme
BP 522
Nouakchott, Mauritania
Tel: + 2222 51502
Fax: + 2222 52894

Ms Bibiane Mbaye Gahamanyi
Administrateur
Union Pour l'Etude de la Population
Africaine
BP 21007 Dakar Ponty
Sénégal
Tel: + 221 825 59 51
Fax: + 221 825 59 55
Email: bibiane@cyg.sn

Mr Mwangi Mbuthia
(deceased)

Ms Clotilde Medegan
Magistrat
Association de Femmes Juristes du Benin
04 BP 0331 Cotonou
Benin
Tel: + 229 32 44 43
Fax: + 229 32 27 86

Mr Mbuye Kapuya Meleka
Avocat
Avocats sans Frontiers
733 Av Col EBEYA
BP 15451
Gombe, Kinshasa
Democratic Republic of Congo
Tel: + 243 12 22855
Fax: + 243 12 21 296

*Justice Odette Murara
President
Kigali Court of Appeal
PO Box 101
Kigali, Rwanda
Tel/fax: + 250 78193

Prof Abdelaziz Nouaydi
Lecturer in Law
University of Fez
Residence Makrizi 24
Ropute Ain Chraf-Fes
Fez, Marocco

Mr Kathurima M'Inoti
International Commission of Jurists
(Kenya Section)
PO Box 59743
Nairobi, Kenya
Tel: + 254 2 228614/340592
Fax: + 254 2 34 05 96

Justice Luis Mondlane
Supreme Court of Mozambique
Tribunal Supremo
Av. Vladamir Lenine
103 C. Postal 278
Maputo, Mozambique
Tel: + 258 1 431002/ 423306
Fax: + 258 1 420697

Mr Benfeito Mosso Ramos
Juge à la Cour Supréme
C P 117
Praia, Cap Vert
Tel: + 238 616901
Fax: + 238 611751

Mr Hisham Mubarak
(Deceased)

Lieutenant Colonel Sanglie Ndao
EMGA SCEM/ADM
BP 15913
Dakar-Fann, Senegal
Tel/fax: + 221 821 77 34

Mrs Rosalie Bissa-Bi Nzogho
Magistrat
Conseiller à la Cour Administrative
BP 5529, Libreville, Gabon
Tel: + 241 72 83 71

Mr Ndubisi Obiorah
Huri-Laws
The Human Rights Law Service
PO Box 3169
34 Creek Road, Apapa
Lagos, Nigeria
Tel: + 234 1 587 6706
Fax: + 234 1 587 6876
Email: Huri-laws@alpha.linkserve.com

Dr Rachel-Claire Okani-Abengue
Vice Doyen
Faculté Science Juridique et Politique
University of Yaounde
II BP 1365
Yaounde, Cameroon
Tel: + 237 22 08 36/ 30 47 84
Fax: + 237 22 30 48 26

Mr Ray Onyegu
Co Executive Director
Shelter Rights Initiative
62 Tafawa Balewa Crescent
Surulere, Lagos
Nigeria
Tel/fax: + 2341 835 367
Email: sri.b@rcl.nig.com

Mr Justice Premo
Legal Practitioner
Minkah - Premo & Co
PO Box 14951
Accra, Ghana
Tel: + 233 21 222 649
Fax: + 233 21 226969

Mr Peter Rosenblum
Harvard Human Rights Program
Harvard Law School
Pound Hall 401
Cambridge, MA 02138
USA
Tel: + 1 617 495 9362
Fax: + 1 617 495 1110
Email: prosenbl@law.harvard.edu

Mr Amadou Sakho
Conseiller Juridique
Ministere Juridique
BP 564
Guinee Conakry
Tel: + 224 41 29 60
Fax: + 224 41 16 17

*Mr Amir Salem
Executive Director
Legal Research and Resources Centre for
Human Rights in Egypt
7 Al Higar St
Roxi Heliopolis
Cairo, Egypt
Tel: + 202 245 209 77
Fax: + 202 259 66 22

Mr Ebrima Sall
Programme Officer
CODESRIA
BP 3304
Dakar, Sénégal
Tel/fax + 221 824 12 89

Ms Lucrecia Seafield
Project Officer
European Foundation for Human Rights
1141 Burnette Street
Hatfield , Pretoria 0028
Tel: + 27 12 32 641
Fax: + 27 12 34 29 059
Email: lucrecia@eufound.org.za

Mr Yosias Tadesse
40 Daleview Road
London, N15 6PJ, UK
Tel: + 44 171 278 2662

*Mr Paulos Tesfagiorgis
55 Abune Yared Street
Asmara, Eritrea
Tel: + 291 1 120 671
Fax: + 29 1 120 195
Emai: paulosba@bt.gemel.com.er

*Professor Ernest Wamba Dia Wamba
Dept of History
UDSM
PO Box 53050
Dar-es-Salaam
Tanzania
Tel: + 255 51 436 72
Fax: + 255 51 43395
Email: wamba@ud.co.tz

Ms Muthoni Lynn Wanyeki
Executive Director
Femnet
PO Box 54562
Nairobi, Kenya
Tel: + 254 2 741 301/741320
Fax: + 254 2 742 927
Email: femnet@africaonline.co.ke

Dr Markus Weilenmann
Buero fuer Kongfliktforschung in
Entwicklungsländern
Alpenstrasse 25
CH-8803 Rueschlikon
Tel: + 0041 17 24 39 39
or 0041 17 24 24 46
Fax: + 0041 17 24 39 40
Email: drmweilenmann@access.ch

Ms Veronic Wright
Commerical Crime Unit
Legal & Constitutional Affairs Division
Commonwealth Secretariat
Pall Mall, London
SW1Y 5HX, UK
Tel: + 44 171 747 6417

AFRONET

Mr Ngande Mwanajiti
Executive Director

Ms Dorah Chisambi
Administrator

AFRONET
BP 31145
Lusaka, Zambia

Tel: + 260 125 1814
Fax: + 260 125 1776
Email: afronet@zamnet.zm

RADDHO

Waly Coly Faye, Secretarie General

Mr Aboubacry Mbodj
Secretaire Administratif

Mr Diedonne Pandare
President Commission Scientifique

Mr Amadou Aly Kane
Ms Ouleye Demba Deme
Ms Oulimata Gaye
Mr Wagane Faye
Mr Karim Cisse
Mr Abdourahmane Dianko
Ms Mame Bassine Niang
Ms Malle Mbow

RADDHO
Rencontre Africaine Pour La Defense des
Droits de L'Homme
Sicap Amitie II
Villa 4024
Allees Seydou Nourou Tall
BP 15246
Dakar, Sénégal
Tel: + 221 824 60 56
Fax: + 221 824 60 52
Email: raddho@telecomplus.sn

INTERIGHTS

Ms Emma Playfair
Executive Director

Mr Chidi Anselm Odinkalu
Senior Legal Officer

Mr Ibrahima Kane
Legal Officer

Ms Romana Cacchioli
Programme Assistant

Ms Fauzia Sheriff
Consultant

INTERIGHTS
Lancaster House
33 Islington High Street
London N1 9LH
UK

Tel: + 44 171 278 32 30
Fax: + 44 171 278 43 34
Email: IR@interights.org

* Participants unable to attend the
meeting in Dakar due to industrial action
by workers at air traffic control Dakar.